Going Local with "Farley"

by Phil Frank

Foreword by Charles Schulz

TEN SPEED PRESS
Berkeley, California

TEN SPEED PRESS
P. O. Box 7123
Berkeley, California 94707

First printing, 1991

Cover design by Fifth Street Design
Text design and book production by Hal Hershey

Special thanks to North American Syndicate/King Features and the *San Francisco Chronicle* where these strips first appeared.

ISBN 0-89815-441-3

Library of Congress Catalog Number 91-050658

Printed in the United States of America

1   2   3   4   5   —   95   94   93   92   91

Foreword

For me, the most important element in a comic strip is still the drawing. Phil Frank's cartooning style has real "bounce." Every figure and every object, whether a background cable car or a window in an apartment, is alive. In other words, the strip is fun to look at. All the writing in the world will not save a comic strip that isn't fun to look at.

Now, as to his material, it is a source of complete amazement to me that he can cartoon the daily happenings of all of us in the Bay Area. It took real courage to accept the challenge to do this kind of feature, and he has my total admiration. Oh, and I almost forgot . . . he draws wonderful animals and funny little kids.

Charles M. Schulz

© 1958 United Feature Syndicate, Inc.

·Introduction·

If there is any single word that comes to mind when I think of my comic strip's sixteen-year life span, it is the word "evolution." *Farley* has moved through as many stages as an amoeba evolving into a circuit court judge.

When first syndicated in 1975, the strip was called *Travels With Farley*. My lead character, a quiet soul with a backpack who wandered the land, acted as a sounding board for the many characters he encountered: the bears at Asphalt State Park; the head ranger, Horace Malone; a guru guide, Baba Re Bop; and a clumsy Pentagon official, Major Mishap.

As times changed, the wandering backpacker became an anachronism. I made him a reporter for *The Daily Demise*. He rented an apartment in a metropolitan environment. The previous tenant left his pet, a loud-mouthed raven named Bruce, who became a permanent fixture. Farley fell in and out of love, covered stories, and appeared in a tidy number of papers from Seattle to Sarasota.

The drawback of syndication is the four- to five-week lead time required between when a strip is drawn and when it actually appears. Issues can change noticeably over a five-week period. That, and the other requirement that the humor be general enough to be comprehended in Tucson or Tuscaloosa, began to take the fun out of cartooning for me.

While I was drawing the strip I was living on a houseboat in Sausalito and became involved in local politics. The editor of the local weekly *Marinscope* suggested I draw a strip for the paper; subject matter would be open, space unlimited, and turnaround time between finished art and the newspaper in the reader's hands was twenty-four hours. For seven years I drew that local feature under the pen name Fritz Crackers (in exchange for free photocopying at the newspaper's offices) and had more fun than I'd ever experienced with national syndication.

The longer I drew the overnight cartoon for the local paper, the harder it became to draw the national strip for the syndicate. I made an appointment with the editor of the *San Francisco Chronicle* and offered to take Farley out of syndication, move him to San Francisco, and let him cover all the great local material that was begging for political comment. I proposed that for one month I turn in six strips that would be hypothetically run the following week. So, for four weeks I drew *Travels With Farley* for national syndication, my second strip *Miles to Go* (which included a Sunday color strip), and the localized *Farley* concept. I was pretty exhausted by the end of the month but it showed the editors that there was ample material for local comment.

I've never regretted the move. I submit a strip and in twelve hours it will be printed in the paper. Since going local, I now get material through a hundred "sources" at the paper, city hall, local government agencies, and many loyal readers. The strip is located in the more widely read news section of the paper. I still have access to 800,000 readers and, if I wish, I can work in the inspiring hubbub of the *Chronicle* newsroom, rather than in the isolation of a studio.

This has not been a one-person operation. For the first two years of the localized *Farley*, Joe Troise, a freelance writer and friend, worked with me on the weekly storyline until I got into the swing of local humor. My wife, Susan, and kids-turned-adults, Stacy and Phil, have supplied ideas and themes that have gotten me out of some pretty tight deadline spots.

Many thanks to them and to the dedicated readers whose letters, calls, and faxes have sparked many of the cartoons contained herein!

GOING LOCAL

In 1985, after 10 years of national syndication with my comic strip "Travels With Farley" I was wanting a change. Humor for national syndication required a generic joke that could be understood in Portland, Maine and Portland, Oregon. Material had to be in to the publisher a month before it ran so it was difficult if not impossible to do timely humor.

I saw so much good material in the local papers that was begging for satire. I proposed to the Chronicle that I take the strip out of syndication and do it as a locally focused exclusive of the Chronicle with a lead time cut from a month to overnight. They said yes.. so for six years San Francisco has had its own comic strip, its private, inside joke on the news.

Not all the characters that were in the syndicated version of the **Farley** strip made it into the local cartoon. Farley's editor at the Daily Demise, his landlady and a few other folks who got little reader reaction were left floating out there in cartoon hyperspace as the rest of the crew entered a local orbit..

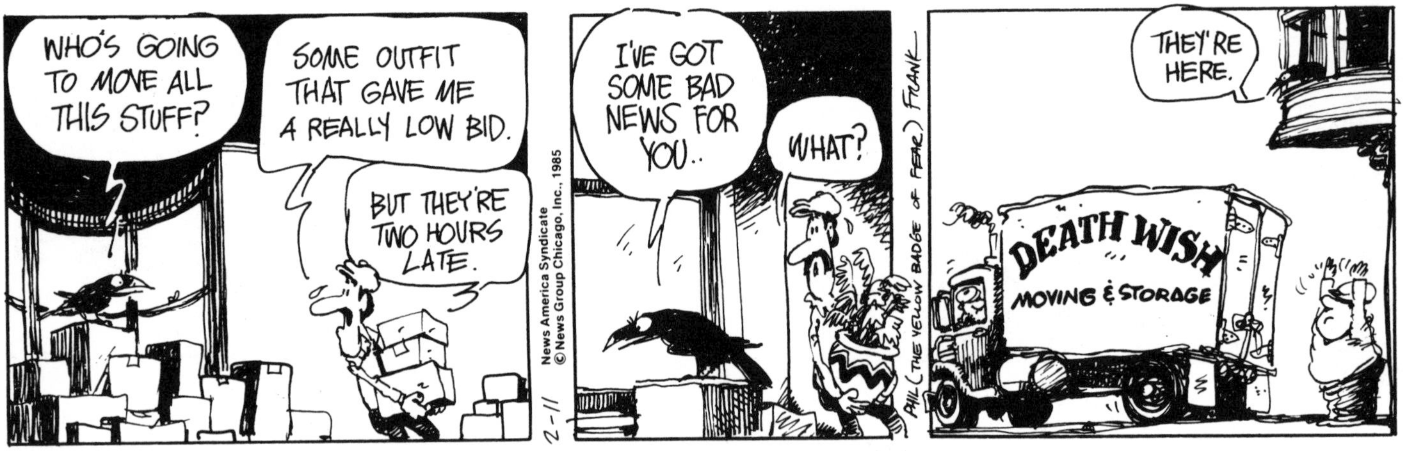
WHO'S GOING TO MOVE ALL THIS STUFF?
SOME OUTFIT THAT GAVE ME A REALLY LOW BID.
BUT THEY'RE TWO HOURS LATE.
2-11
News America Syndicate © News Group Chicago, Inc., 1985
I'VE GOT SOME BAD NEWS FOR YOU..
WHAT?
PHIL (THE YELLOW BADGE OF FEAR) FRANK
THEY'RE HERE.
DEATH WISH
MOVING & STORAGE

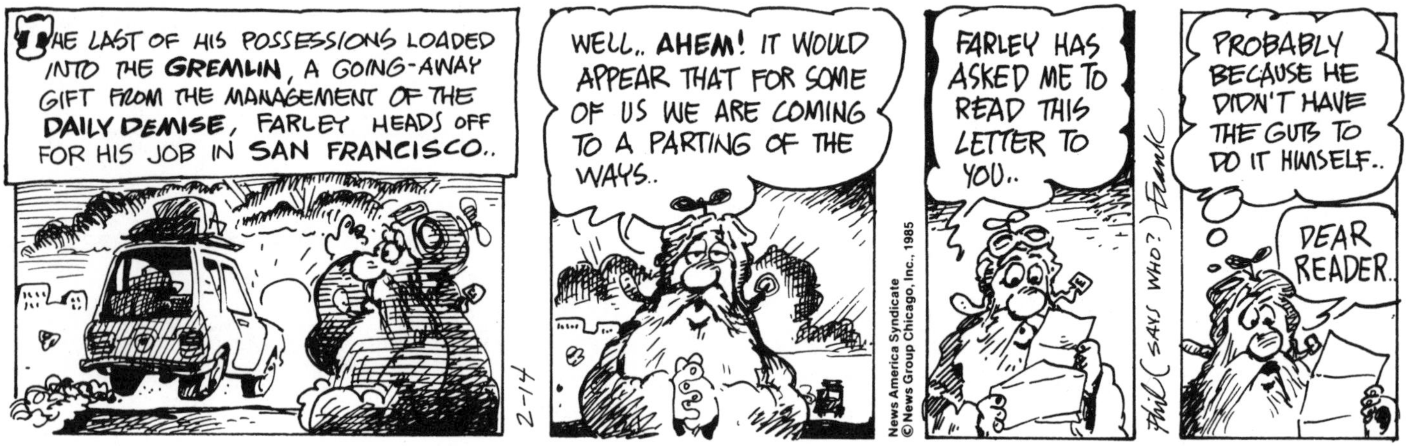
THE LAST OF HIS POSSESSIONS LOADED INTO THE GREMLIN, A GOING-AWAY GIFT FROM THE MANAGEMENT OF THE DAILY DEMISE, FARLEY HEADS OFF FOR HIS JOB IN SAN FRANCISCO..
2-14
WELL.. AHEM! IT WOULD APPEAR THAT FOR SOME OF US WE ARE COMING TO A PARTING OF THE WAYS..
News America Syndicate © News Group Chicago, Inc., 1985
FARLEY HAS ASKED ME TO READ THIS LETTER TO YOU..
Phil (SAYS WHO?) Frank
PROBABLY BECAUSE HE DIDN'T HAVE THE GUTS TO DO IT HIMSELF..
DEAR READER..

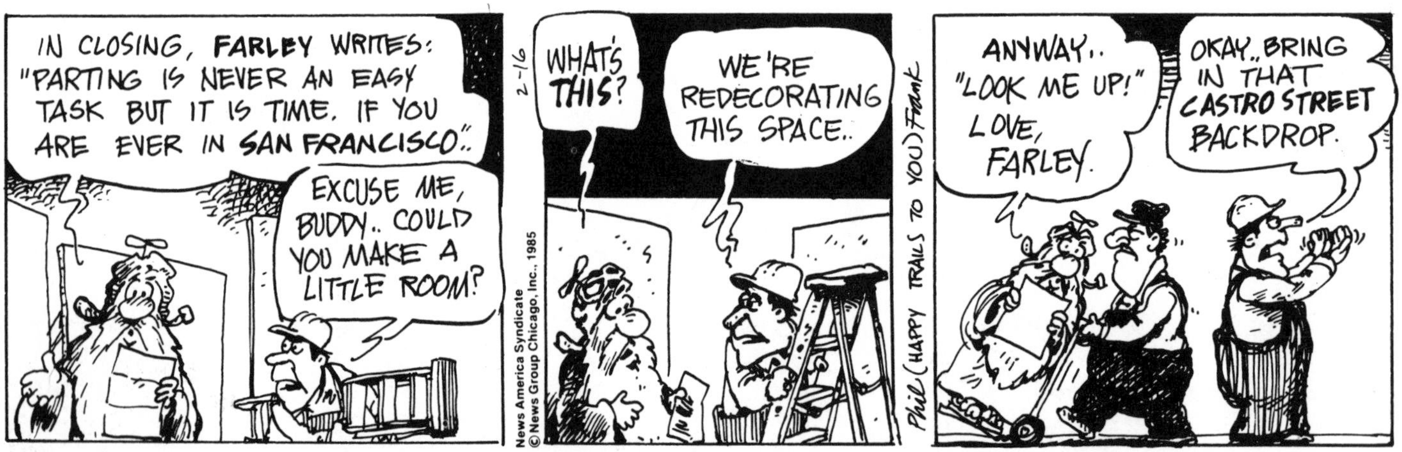
IN CLOSING, FARLEY WRITES: "PARTING IS NEVER AN EASY TASK BUT IT IS TIME. IF YOU ARE EVER IN SAN FRANCISCO"..
EXCUSE ME, BUDDY.. COULD YOU MAKE A LITTLE ROOM?
2-16
News America Syndicate © News Group Chicago, Inc., 1985
WHAT'S THIS?
WE'RE REDECORATING THIS SPACE..
Phil (HAPPY TRAILS TO YOU) Frank
ANYWAY.. "LOOK ME UP!" LOVE, FARLEY.
OKAY.. BRING IN THAT CASTRO STREET BACKDROP.

The next day the strip is appearing exclusively in the Chronicle:

WELCOME TO SAN FRANCISCO, FARLEY... AND TO THE DAILY REQUIREMENT.

A FINE PAPER. I'VE HEARD MANY GREAT THINGS ABOUT THE EDITORIAL EXCELLEN..

GADS! YOU SHOULD'VE BEEN HERE LAST WEEK! THE COPS RAIDED THE MITCHELL BROTHERS THEATER.

IT WAS A JOURNALISTIC FREE-FOR-ALL!

UH.. YES.. I SAW THE LEAD STORY, SIR..

"BIG BUST AT EROTIC THEATER!" I WROTE THAT HEADLINE MYSELF!

LOOK, KID.. YOU'VE JUST GOTTEN TO TOWN.. YOU NEED TO GET LOCATED..

TAKE SOME TIME..

EDITOR

NO SIREE!! I SURE DON'T ENVY YOU.. ..A YOUNG, LONELY, SINGLE GUY IN A BIG CITY..

YOU MAY EVEN BE FORCED TO SHARE A PLACE WITH SOME STRANGER.. MAYBE EVEN A WOMAN..

SOME YOUNG, LONELY, SINGLE..

UH, SIR.. YOUR NAILS ARE DIGGING INTO MY SHOULDER..

I LIKE THIS APARTMENT BETTER THAN THE OTHERS YOU'VE SHOWN ME, BUT..

BUT WHAT?

IT'S ABOUT THE NEIGHBORHOOD.. IT'S PRETTY ROUGH..

WHAT'S TO WORRY? YOU'RE RIGHT NEXT DOOR TO A POLICE STATION!! THERE'S A SQUAD CAR SITTING IN FRONT OF THE PLACE!

BUT.. ITS WHEELS ARE GONE..

TRUE...

EMERGENCY 911

AHA!!

Finding a place for Farley to rent in San Francisco was not too difficult. While he was going through the trauma and drama of apartment hunting in the comic strip, I was out there looking too- for a real place for him to live. While wandering through North Beach one day I spotted an obviously vacant apartment above an Italian bakery on Green Street. Turns out the apartment had been vacant for 20 or 30 years because the building's owner, Fernando, lived on the second floor and didn't want anyone walking around above him. Through interpreters, Fernando agreed that Farley, the cartoon character, could reside upstairs, if he was very quiet.

LOOK, SUE ELLEN!! I'VE GOT A LOVELY APARTMENT BUT NO FURNISHINGS! WHERE ARE THEY??

© Phil Frank 1985.

DO YOU EVER GET THE FEELING THAT WE, AS AMERICANS, ARE TOO ATTACHED TO OUR MATERIAL GOODS? MAYBE WE SHOULD SHED..

DEATH WISH MOVING

3-9

SUE ELLEN! I'M DOWN TO A SLEEPING BAG AND A HUNGRY BIRD. PERSONALLY, I NEED MORE THAN THIS!

Phil (TENDER MERCENARIES) Frank

IT WAS WORTH A TRY..

HELLO? IS THIS DEATH WISH MOVING AND STORAGE? GOOD! I'M CALLING ABOUT MY BELONGINGS.

3-2

© 1985 PHIL FRANK

2.

I WAS TOLD BY THE MOVERS THAT MY GOODS WOULD ARRIVE IN THE BAY AREA IN LATE FEBRUARY.

Phil (IN ONE ERA AND OUT THE OTHER) Frank

.. AND I HAVE THIS WONDERFUL APARTMENT NOW AND I'D..

WHAT?

WELL.. NO.. THEY DIDN'T SAY LATE FEBRUARY OF WHAT YEAR..

I JUST ASSUMED..

IT'S SIX A.M.. FROM THE OVENS OF THE **DANILO BAKERY** THE AROMA OF FRESH BAKED FRENCH BREAD RISES..

..TO AWAKEN THE TENANT IN THE THIRD FLOOR APARTMENT..

OH.. NO!!

SNIFF!! SNIFF!!

"AT SEVEN A.M. THE FOCACCIA GOES INTO THE OVENS..

NOT THE PIZZA BREAD!

WHAT ARE YOU COOKING IN THERE?

GARLIC WAFFLES. WHY?

Phil (FOR PIZZA'S SAKE!) Frank

FARLEY.. I NEVER SAW THE FOLLOW-UP ON THE BEAR SIGHTING AT **GOLDEN GATE PARK**..

ER.. BEAR SIGHTING? OH.. YES..

© Phil Frank 1985

WELL.. I INTERVIEWED ALL THE WITNESSES AND SPOKE WITH THE LOCAL AUTHORITIES..

AND?

THEY'RE LOOKING INTO THE POSSIBILITY OF MASS HALLUCINATIONS..

SO.. HOW DO YOU EXPLAIN THESE PHOTOS OF ROLLERSKATING BEARS IN SOMBREROS?

UH... SWAMP GAS?

Phil (BORN TO LOOT.) Frank

CHIEF.. I'VE TALKED TO THE EXPERTS.. THIS UNDERWATER.. HUM IN SAUSALITO MUST BE A SEWAGE PUMP..

WHY DO YOU INSIST ON PUSHING THE SINGING FISH THEORY?

© Phil Frank 1985

BECAUSE IT SELLS NEWS-PAPERS, THAT'S WHY!! HUMMING FISH SPAWNING BEFORE THEY DIE! IT'S GOT ALL THE ELEMENTS..

MYSTERY.. LOVE, ..DEATH AND ADVENTURE!! **NOW**.. WRITE ME A STORY THAT'LL SELL PAPERS!!

"SINGING SALMON SLAYS SELF"??

EDITOR

Phil (YOU BAIT YOUR LIFE) Frank

"Well.. here we are.. Now what?"

Four of my best characters were a quartet of bears that Farley dealt with each summer at Asphalt State Park. I couldn't leave them behind so I had to find a job for them in the city. I noticed all the trendy eateries popping up around San Francisco but not one that catered to animals... ...until the bears opened the Fog City Dumpster.. where the elite with four feet meet!

I stood transfixed in the gathering darkness of the wharf area south of Market..

© Phil Frank 1985

8-28

The bears were opening their chic new restaurant. I stood amongst raccoons in expensive Italian suits.. Tuxedoed penguins and skunks..

Gourmet leftovers.. ..the final frontier.

FOG CITY (WHY NOT WORRY?) DUMPSTER

Phil (VALET BARKING) Frank

The opening of the bears' chic new restaurant is certainly a big success.

© Phil Frank 1985

SKUNK.. PARTY OF FOUR..

FOG CITY DUMPSTER

Farley surveys the scene from a corner table with Franklin, the manager.

WOULD YOU PREFER TO SIT IN SCENTED OR NON-SCENTED?

Phil (OUT TO BRUNCH BUNCH) Frank

SO I ASKED MYSELF.. WHAT DO THE ANIMALS OF THIS CITY NEED? A PLACE TO SEE AND BE SEEN !!

ISN'T THAT MORRIS THE CAT'S WIDOW?

I VANT TO BE ALONE.

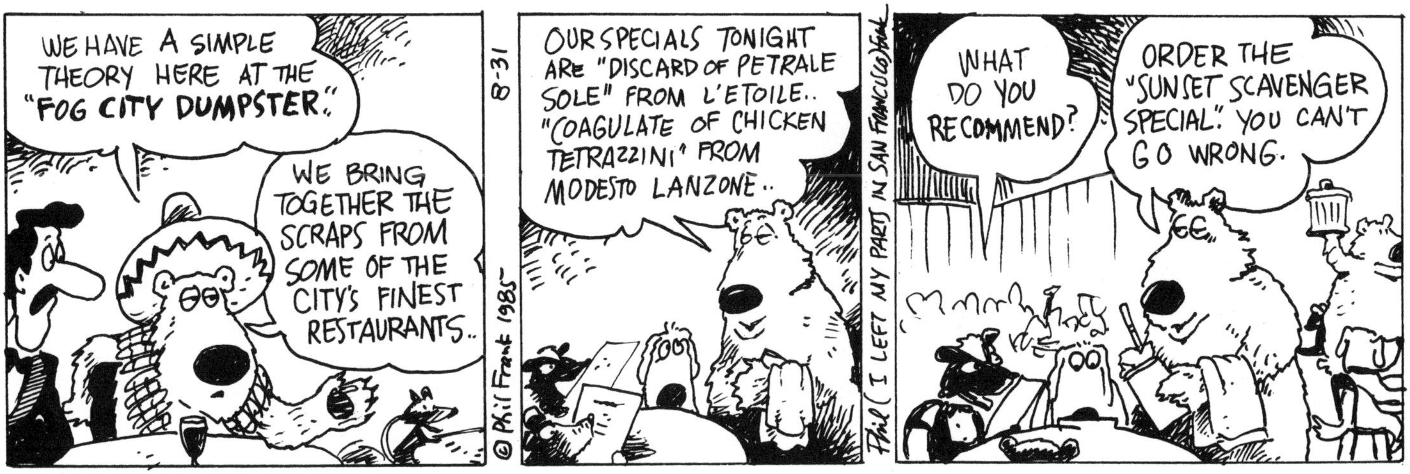
WE HAVE A SIMPLE THEORY HERE AT THE "FOG CITY DUMPSTER".
WE BRING TOGETHER THE SCRAPS FROM SOME OF THE CITY'S FINEST RESTAURANTS..
8-31
© Phil Frank 1985
OUR SPECIALS TONIGHT ARE "DISCARD OF PETRALE SOLE" FROM L'ETOILE.. "COAGULATE OF CHICKEN TETRAZZINI" FROM MODESTO LANZONE..
Phil (I LEFT MY PARTS IN SAN FRANCISCO) Frank
WHAT DO YOU RECOMMEND?
ORDER THE "SUNSET SCAVENGER SPECIAL". YOU CAN'T GO WRONG.

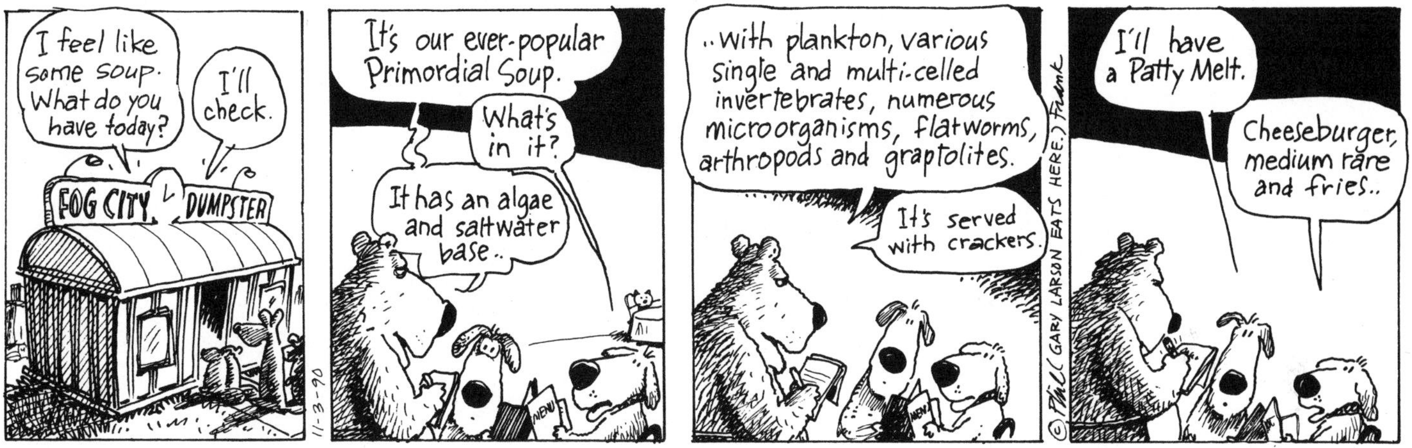
I feel like some soup. What do you have today?
I'll check.
FOG CITY DUMPSTER
11-3-90
It's our ever-popular Primordial Soup.
What's in it?
It has an algae and saltwater base..
..with plankton, various single and multi-celled invertebrates, numerous microorganisms, flatworms, arthropods and graptolites.
It's served with crackers.
© Phil (GARY LARSON EATS HERE.) Frank
I'll have a Patty Melt.
Cheeseburger, medium rare and fries..

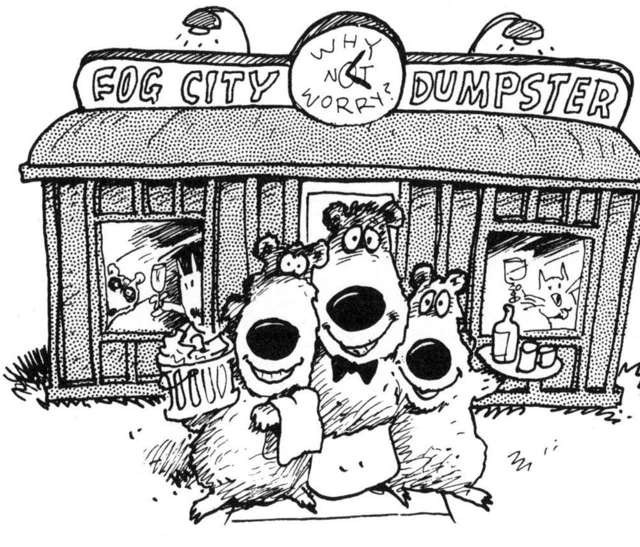
FOG CITY
WHY NOT WORRY?
DUMPSTER

For seven months the localized strip ran in the comics section of the paper, where it had appeared for 10 years. I drew upon local material for the subject matter but since the comics page was "locked up" (ready for print) a week before it ran, it was impossible to be right on top of the news.

One day, Bill German, the editor, gave me the good news that the strip was moving to the "jump page" in the news section. Now I could deliver a strip the night before it was on the doorsteps of 800,000 readers. For a couple of weeks prior to the first "jump page" strip, the paper had been running numerous diagrams of President Reagan's digestive tract on that page. He was having some suspicious polyps removed. Hence....

FARLEY.. I'M MOVING YOUR COLUMN TODAY.. I THINK YOUR STUFF IS TOO GOOD TO BURY..

GEE.. THANKS, CHIEF.

© Phil Frank 1985

9-30

YOU'LL GO TO THE JUMP PAGE. IT'S WHERE THE FRONT PAGE STORIES WRAP UP.. IT'S REAL COLORFUL.. USUALLY A DISASTER PHOTO OR TWO AND LOTS OF MAPS AND DIAGRAMS..

I'M HONORED.

Frank (NURSE OF STEEL)

WHO ELSE GETS TO KEEP COMPANY WITH CROSS-SECTIONS OF THE PRESIDENT'S LOWER DIGESTIVE TRACT?

EDITOR

Now I could **really** play with the readers' minds! Lottery numbers would be picked at 8 p.m.... next morning they'd be in the "Farley" strip. A headline story on the front page would often wrap up on the jump page — next to a cartoon on the same subject.

HOLD THE PRESS!!

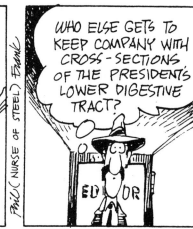

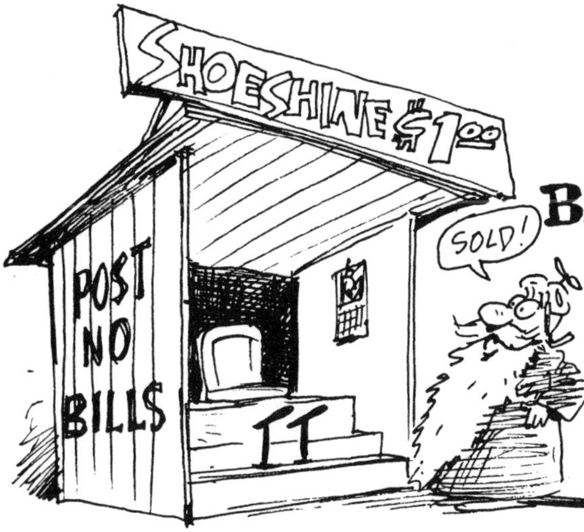
SHOESHINE $1.00
POST NO BILLS
SOLD!

Baba made the transition from national to local. He was perfect to comment on the New Age scene with its Bay Area "head" quarters. He needed an office. I'd noticed an abandoned shoe shine shack displaced by the construction of the Nordstrom store at Fifth and Market so I made it Baba's intergalactic headquarters.

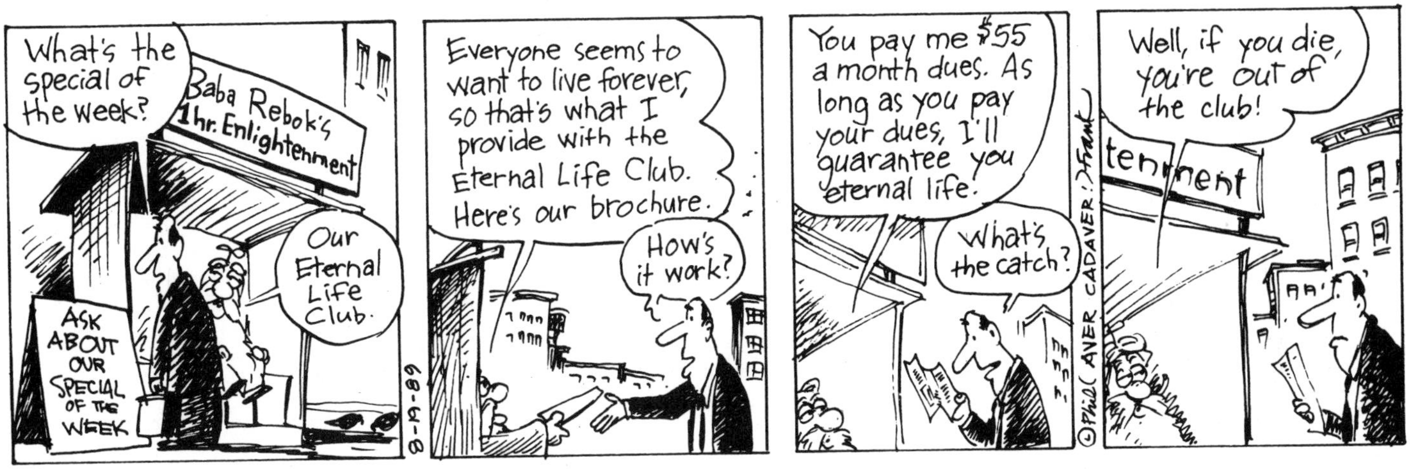
What's the special of the week?
Baba Rebok's 1hr. Enlightenment
ASK ABOUT OUR SPECIAL OF THE WEEK
Our Eternal Life Club.
8-19-89
Everyone seems to want to live forever, so that's what I provide with the Eternal Life Club. Here's our brochure.
How's it work?
You pay me $55 a month dues. As long as you pay your dues, I'll guarantee you eternal life.
What's the catch?
©Phil (CAVER CADAVER!) Frank
Well, if you die, you're out of the club!

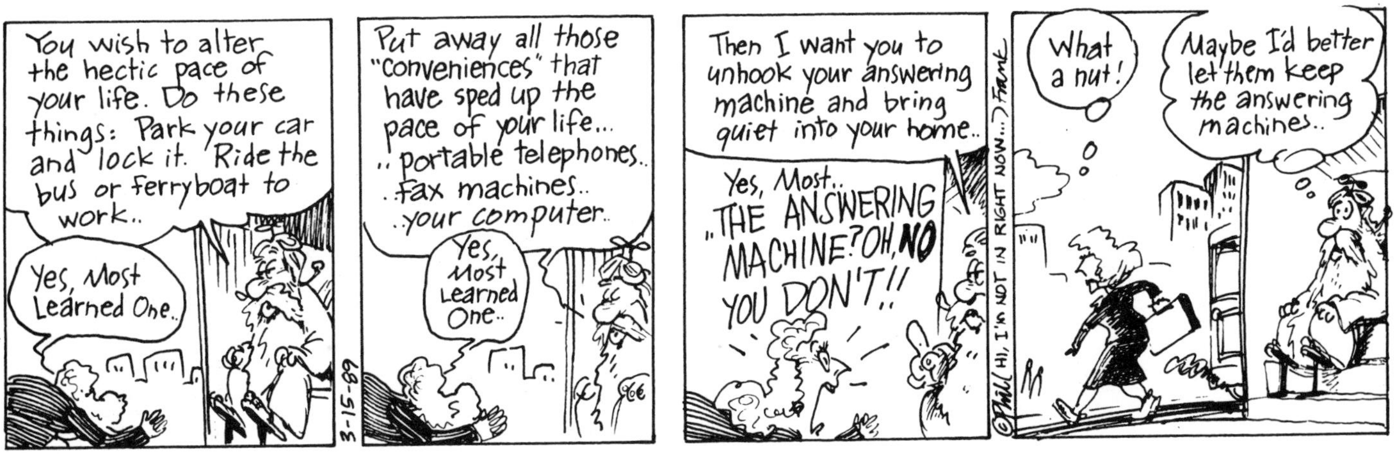
You wish to alter the hectic pace of your life. Do these things: Park your car and lock it. Ride the bus or ferryboat to work..
Yes, Most Learned One..
3-15-89
Put away all those "conveniences" that have sped up the pace of your life... ..portable telephones.. ..fax machines.. ..your computer..
Yes, Most Learned One..
Then I want you to unhook your answering machine and bring quiet into your home..
Yes, Most.. ..THE ANSWERING MACHINE? OH, NO YOU DON'T!!
©Phil (HI, I'M NOT IN RIGHT NOW...) Frank
What a nut!
Maybe I'd better let them keep the answering machines..

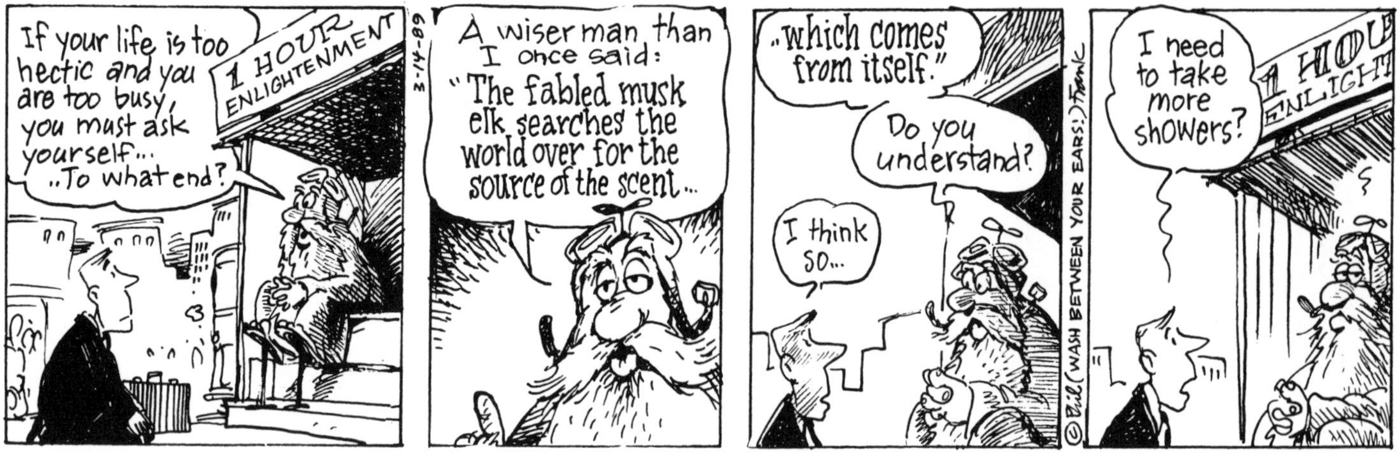
If your life is too hectic and you are too busy, you must ask yourself... ..To what end?
1 HOUR ENLIGHTENMENT
3-14-89
A wiser man than I once said: "The fabled musk elk searches the world over for the source of the scent...
..which comes from itself."
Do you understand?
I think so...
© Bill (WASH BETWEEN YOUR EARS!) Frank
I need to take more showers?
1 HOU ENLIGHT

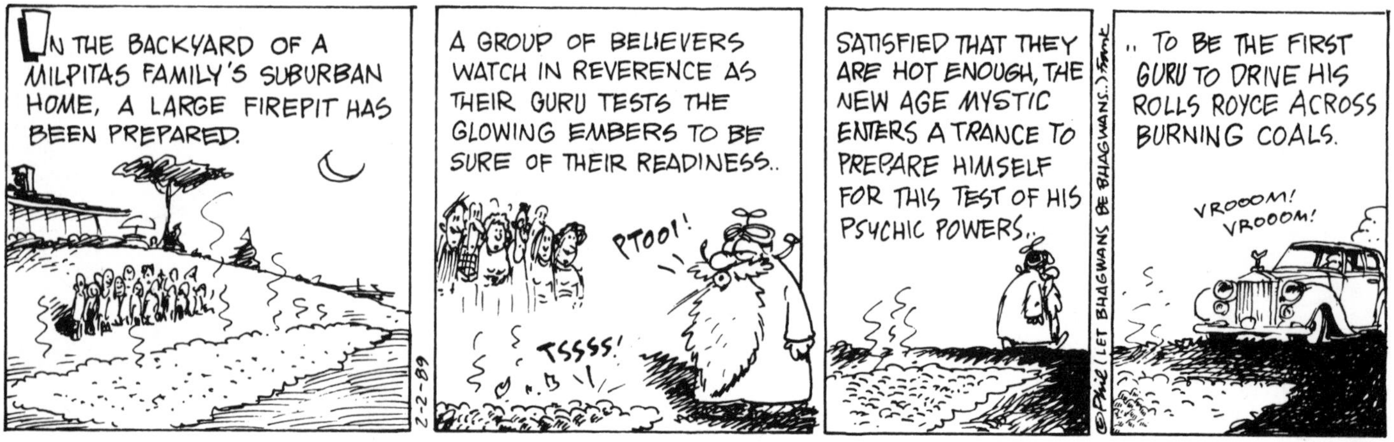
IN THE BACKYARD OF A MILPITAS FAMILY'S SUBURBAN HOME, A LARGE FIREPIT HAS BEEN PREPARED.
2-2-89
A GROUP OF BELIEVERS WATCH IN REVERENCE AS THEIR GURU TESTS THE GLOWING EMBERS TO BE SURE OF THEIR READINESS..
PTOO!
TSSSS!
SATISFIED THAT THEY ARE HOT ENOUGH, THE NEW AGE MYSTIC ENTERS A TRANCE TO PREPARE HIMSELF FOR THIS TEST OF HIS PSYCHIC POWERS..
© Phil (LET BHAGWANS BE BHAGWANS.) Frank
.. TO BE THE FIRST GURU TO DRIVE HIS ROLLS ROYCE ACROSS BURNING COALS.
VROOOM! VROOOM!

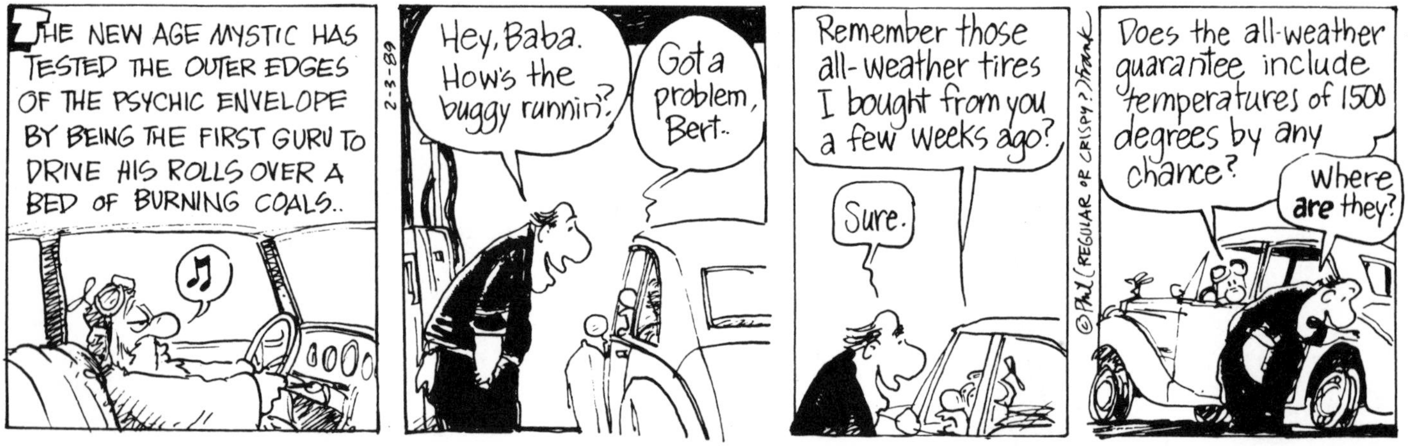
THE NEW AGE MYSTIC HAS TESTED THE OUTER EDGES OF THE PSYCHIC ENVELOPE BY BEING THE FIRST GURU TO DRIVE HIS ROLLS OVER A BED OF BURNING COALS..
2-3-89
Hey, Baba. How's the buggy runnin'?
Got a problem, Bert..
Remember those all-weather tires I bought from you a few weeks ago?
Sure.
© Phil (REGULAR OR CRISPY?) Frank
Does the all-weather guarantee include temperatures of 1500 degrees by any chance?
Where **are** they?

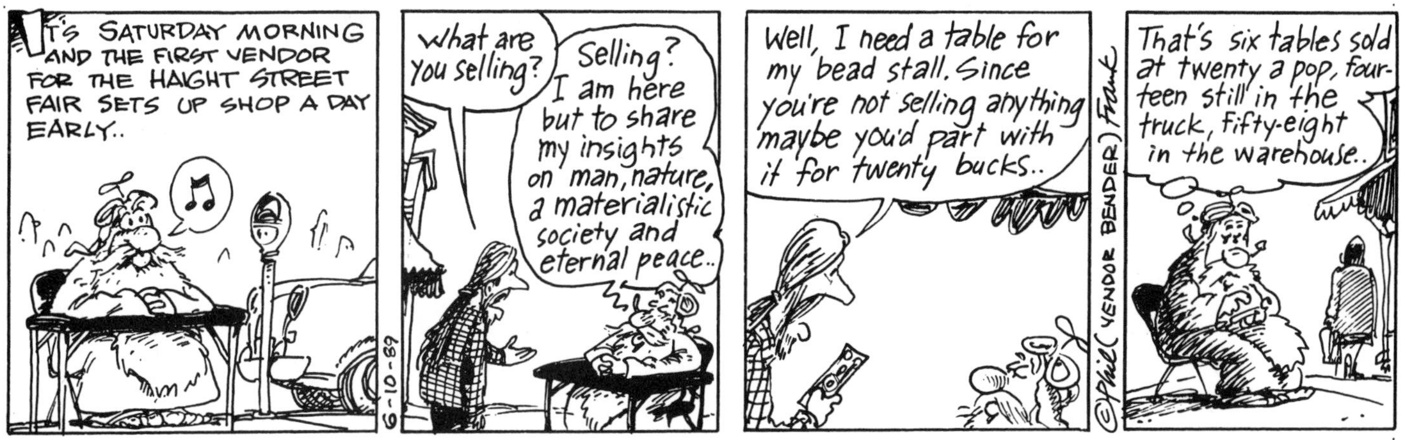
IT'S SATURDAY MORNING AND THE FIRST VENDOR FOR THE HAIGHT STREET FAIR SETS UP SHOP A DAY EARLY..
6-10-89
What are you selling?
Selling? I am here but to share my insights on man, nature, a materialistic society and eternal peace..
Well, I need a table for my bead stall. Since you're not selling anything maybe you'd part with it for twenty bucks..
© Phil (VENDOR BENDER) Frank
That's six tables sold at twenty a pop, fourteen still in the truck, fifty-eight in the warehouse..

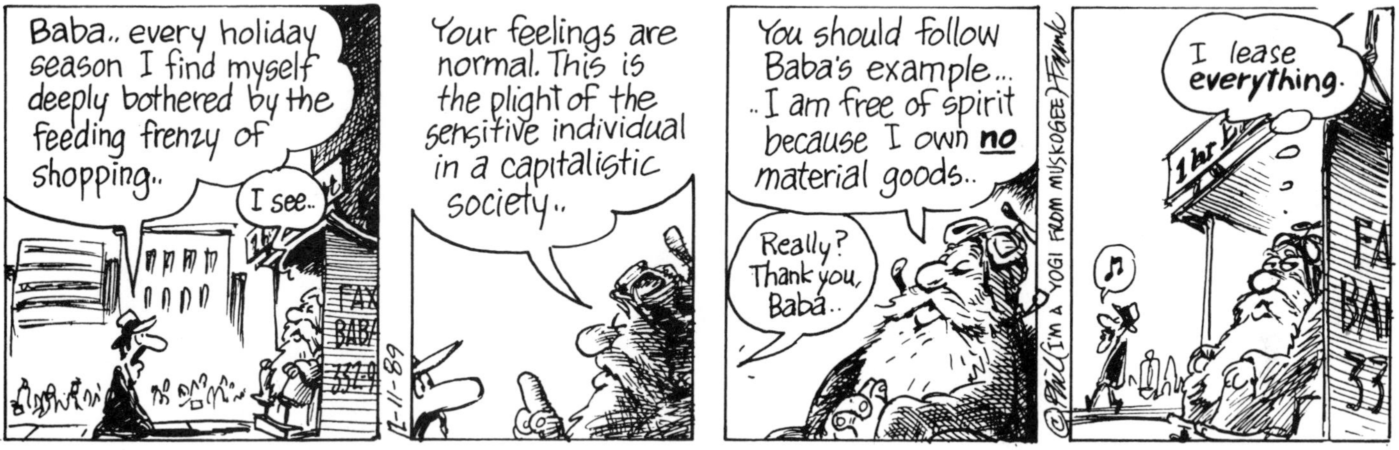
Baba.. every holiday season I find myself deeply bothered by the feeding frenzy of shopping..
I see..
12-11-89
Your feelings are normal. This is the plight of the sensitive individual in a capitalistic society..
You should follow Baba's example... ..I am free of spirit because I own **no** material goods..
Really? Thank you, Baba..
© Phil (I'M A YOGI FROM MUSKOGEE) Frank
I lease **everything**.

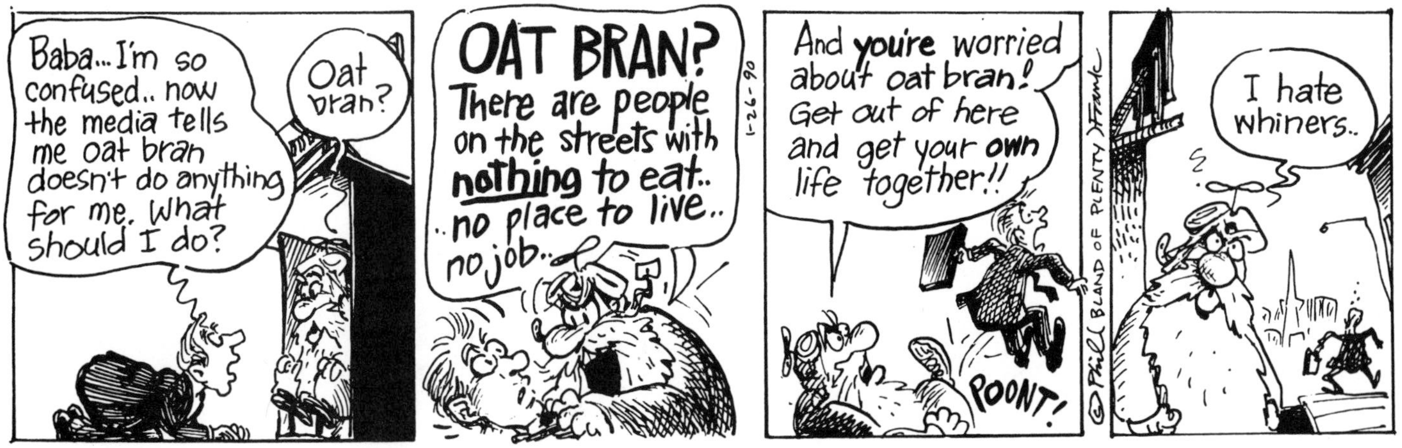
Baba... I'm so confused.. now the media tells me oat bran doesn't do anything for me. What should I do?
Oat bran?
OAT BRAN? There are people on the streets with nothing to eat.. no place to live.. no job..
1-26-90
And **you're** worried about oat bran! Get out of here and get your **own** life together!!
POONT!
© Phil (BLAND OF PLENTY) Frank
I hate whiners..

Inspector Tuslo is no Sam Spade but **is** a new character since the strip went local. I needed a slightly bumbling source inside the police department as a contact for Farley. Tuslo drives an unmarked police car and covers the cocaine busts and political corruption of San Francisco. And then, sometimes it covers him.

INSPECTOR TUSLO'S THE NAME. I WAS WORKING NARCOTICS UNDERCOVER IN NORTH BEACH. I HAD A DIVE STAKED OUT.

UNMARKED POLICE CAR

12-22-88

I MADE MY WAY CAUTIOUSLY TO THE BACK DOOR OF THE SHOP. I WAS SURE THE PLACE WAS A FRONT (EVEN THOUGH I **WAS** AT THE BACK). THIS WAS MY CHANCE TO PROVE IT.

YEAH?

Buon giorno! Guido sent me. I want to make a buy. A kilo of Colombian.

©Phil (A-KILO-WHAT?) Frank

DRAT! TWO MORE POUNDS OF COFFEE BEANS!

THE BACK SEAT OF INSPECTOR TUSLO'S UNMARKED POLICE CAR WAS BEGINNING TO FILL UP WITH BAGS OF COFFEE BEANS.

UNMARKED POLICE CAR

FOR THREE WEEKS HE'D BEEN WORKING NARCOTICS DETAIL IN NORTH BEACH, TRYING TO MAKE COCAINE BUYS..

12-23-88

BUT EVERY TIME HE TRIED TO BUY A KILO OF THE BEST COLOMBIAN HE ENDED UP WITH COFFEE BEANS.

DRAT!

©Phil (NO GROUNDS FOR INDICTMENT) Frank

EITHER THE NORTH BEACH COCAINE CARTEL HAS BEEN BROKEN OR HIS COVER HAS BEEN BLOWN.

Hey, man.. I got a five-pound jar of Folger's crystals if you're interested.

Get lost!

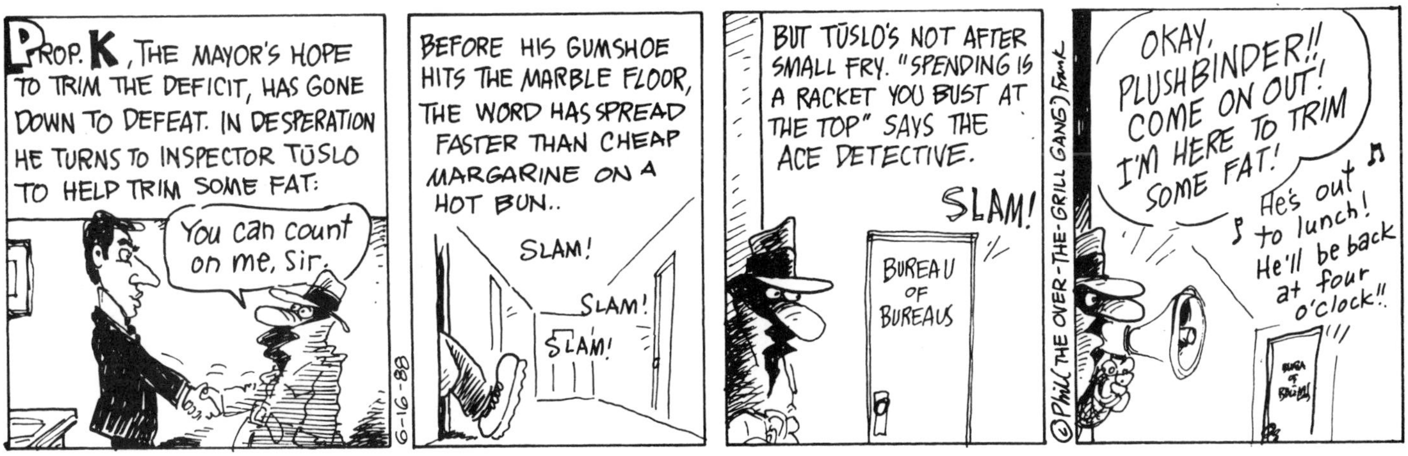
PROP. K, THE MAYOR'S HOPE TO TRIM THE DEFICIT, HAS GONE DOWN TO DEFEAT. IN DESPERATION HE TURNS TO INSPECTOR TŪSLO TO HELP TRIM SOME FAT:
You can count on me, Sir.
6-16-88
BEFORE HIS GUMSHOE HITS THE MARBLE FLOOR, THE WORD HAS SPREAD FASTER THAN CHEAP MARGARINE ON A HOT BUN..
SLAM!
SLAM!
SLAM!
BUT TŪSLO'S NOT AFTER SMALL FRY. "SPENDING IS A RACKET YOU BUST AT THE TOP" SAYS THE ACE DETECTIVE.
SLAM!
BUREAU OF BUREAUS
© Phil (THE OVER-THE-GRILL GANG) Frank
OKAY, PLUSHBINDER!! COME ON OUT! I'M HERE TO TRIM SOME FAT!
He's out to lunch! He'll be back at four o'clock!!

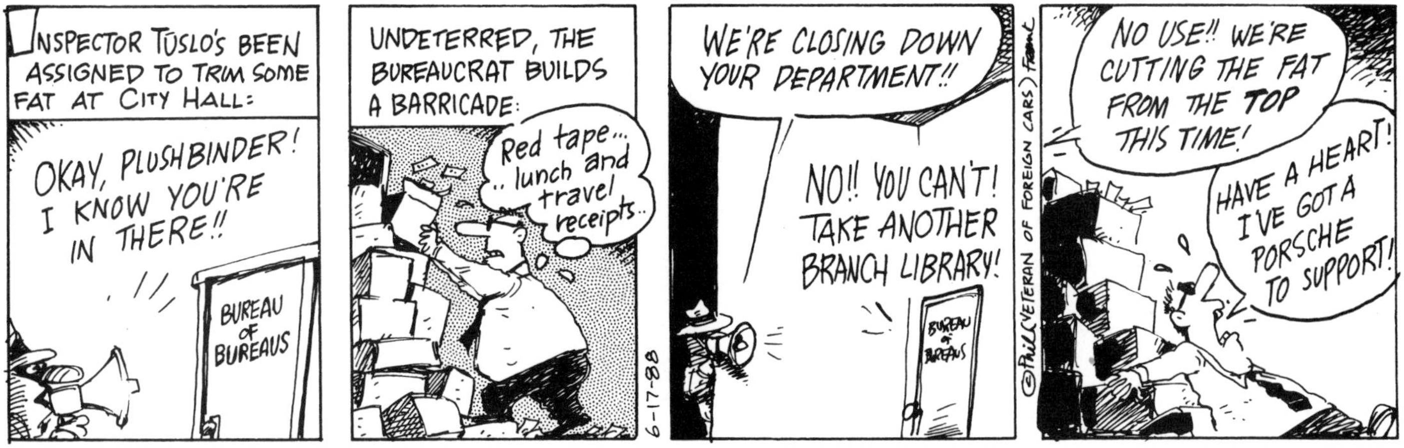
INSPECTOR TŪSLO'S BEEN ASSIGNED TO TRIM SOME FAT AT CITY HALL:
OKAY, PLUSHBINDER! I KNOW YOU'RE IN THERE!!
BUREAU OF BUREAUS
UNDETERRED, THE BUREAUCRAT BUILDS A BARRICADE:
Red tape... ..lunch and travel receipts..
6-17-88
WE'RE CLOSING DOWN YOUR DEPARTMENT!!
NO!! YOU CAN'T! TAKE ANOTHER BRANCH LIBRARY!
BUREAU OF BUREAUS
© Phil (VETERAN OF FOREIGN CARS) Frank
NO USE!! WE'RE CUTTING THE FAT FROM THE TOP THIS TIME!
HAVE A HEART! I'VE GOT A PORSCHE TO SUPPORT!

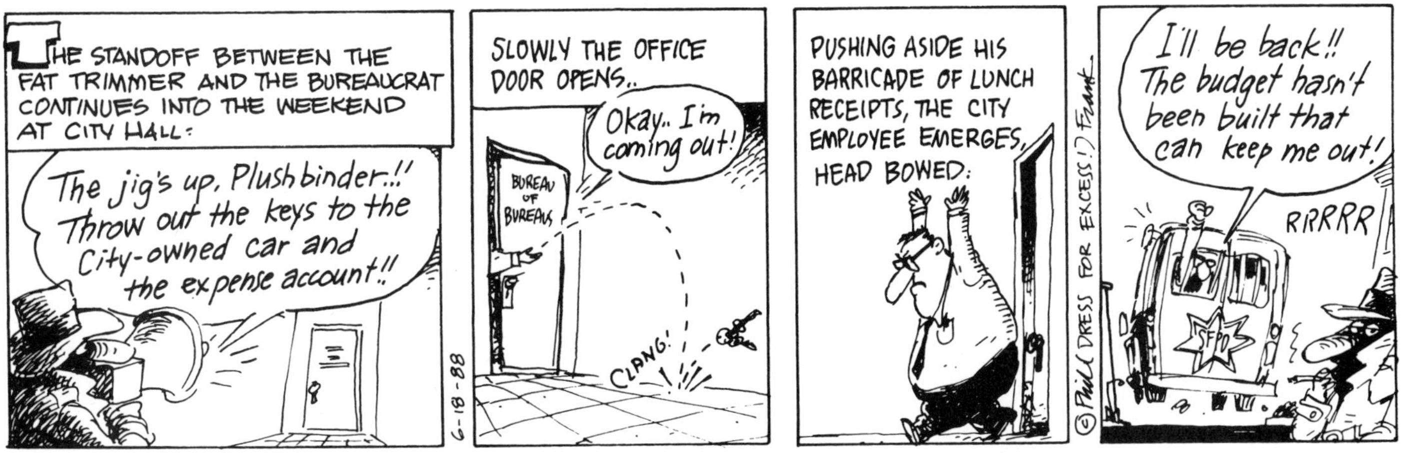
THE STANDOFF BETWEEN THE FAT TRIMMER AND THE BUREAUCRAT CONTINUES INTO THE WEEKEND AT CITY HALL:
The jig's up, Plushbinder..!! Throw out the keys to the City-owned car and the expense account!!
6-18-88
SLOWLY THE OFFICE DOOR OPENS..
Okay.. I'm coming out!
BUREAU OF BUREAUS
CLANG!
PUSHING ASIDE HIS BARRICADE OF LUNCH RECEIPTS, THE CITY EMPLOYEE EMERGES, HEAD BOWED:
© Phil (DRESS FOR EXCESS!) Frank
I'll be back!! The budget hasn't been built that can keep me out!
RRRRR
SFPD

I'D BEEN TAILING THIS SELF-CENTERED WHELP FOR THREE DAYS. FINALLY I'D CORNERED HIM IN A LOCAL EATERY...

THERE HE SAT WITH HIS PORTABLE PHONE, LAP-TOP COMPUTER AND HIS FAX MACHINE... TOTALLY OBLIVIOUS OF THE OTHER PATRONS WHO'D COME THERE TO EAT..

LOOK, BARRY.. OFFER HIM A TOTAL BUY OUT!

Inspector Tuslo, S.F.P.D. Bad Manners Squad. I've got a warrant for your arrest, scum!

Uh.. let me get back to you, Barry...

3-24-89

© Phil (LOOK OUT! HE'S GOT A PEN!) Frank

What's the charge?

Impersonating an office. Let's go!

Ahem! I have information here for **Frugal Faucet** about improprieties involving certain Water Department officials..

Why are you giving them to me, Tuslo?

2-23-90

"I've heard that you might have..er.. access to him... you know... "Who, disguised as a mild-mannered reporter for major metropolitan newspaper.."

WINK! WINK!

I'm sorry, Inspector. Can't help you..

Too bad.. these are very compromising photos..

© Phil (Faster than a speeding bullet.) Frank

I'll see that he gets them!

GRRRRR..

The Golden Gate Bridge board, with its busses, ferries, 50th anniversary celebration and ever-increasing tolls, had been the focus of much news coverage. I needed one character to involve in all the bridge stories so I created a new employee, one G. Gordon Khan (G for Genghis), who wears a suit over his obviously barbarian attitudes. He's been a consistently popular character except at the Golden Gate Bridge District offices!

INSIDE THE SLEEPING YURT SET UP IN HIS NOE VALLEY BACKYARD..

ZZZZ

"GENGHIS GORDON KHAN, GOLDEN GATE BRIDGE DIRECTOR, DREAMS PEACEFULLY..

$1... $2... $3..

ONE MUST WONDER WHAT COULD BRING SUCH PLEASURE TO HIS COUNTENANCE..

$4... $5... $6.

$7... $8... $9.

©PAUL (SHEEP AT TWICE THE PRICE) FRANK

THE GOLDEN GATE BRIDGE DISTRICT MEETS TO DISCUSS A SENSITIVE ISSUE.

The chair recognizes G. Gordon Khan..

In the past we have often been at odds, but I rise now in support of a second deck on the bridge for rail service.

Thank you, Genghis..

As you know, noted authorities throughout history have proven trains can be profitable.

Like Jesse James.

©PAUL (NO TRAINING NECESSARY) FRANK

Your attention please! There's been a slight fare increase!

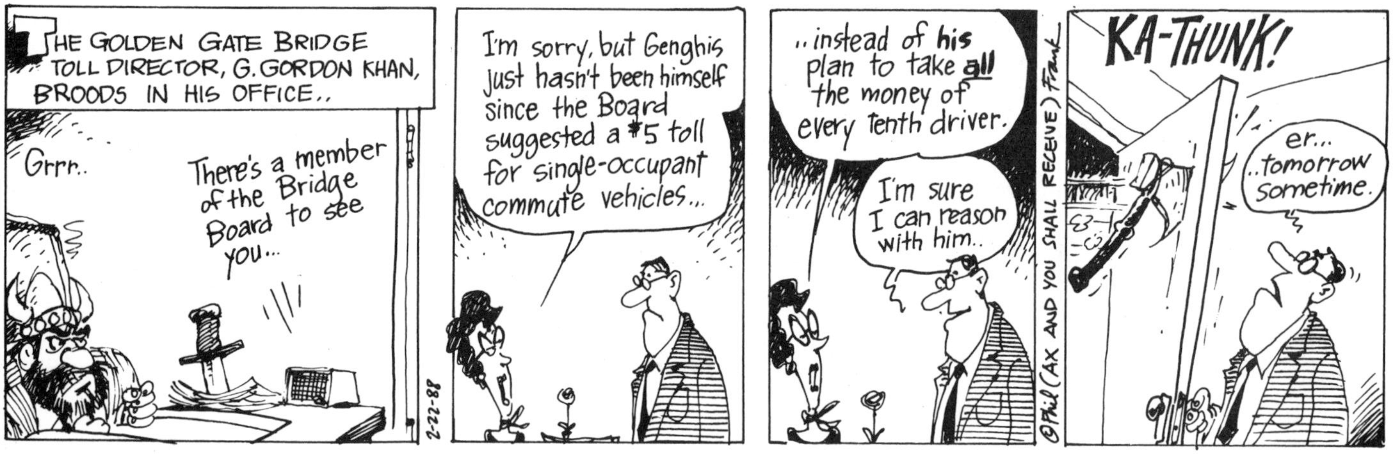
THE GOLDEN GATE BRIDGE TOLL DIRECTOR, G. GORDON KHAN, BROODS IN HIS OFFICE..
Grrr..
There's a member of the Bridge Board to see you...
2-22-88
I'm sorry, but Genghis just hasn't been himself since the Board suggested a $5 toll for single-occupant commute vehicles...
.. instead of **his** plan to take **all** the money of every tenth driver.
I'm sure I can reason with him..
©Phil (AX AND YOU SHALL RECEIVE) Frank
KA-THUNK!
er... ..tomorrow sometime.

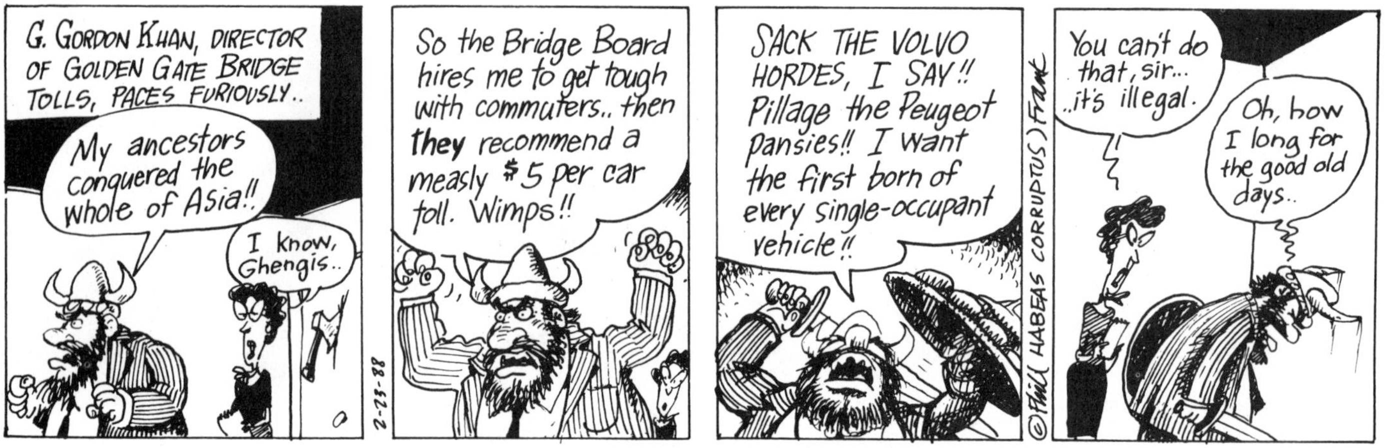
G. GORDON KHAN, DIRECTOR OF GOLDEN GATE BRIDGE TOLLS, PACES FURIOUSLY..
My ancestors conquered the whole of Asia!!
I know, Ghengis..
2-23-88
So the Bridge Board hires me to get tough with commuters.. then **they** recommend a measly $5 per car toll. Wimps!!
SACK THE VOLVO HORDES, I SAY!! Pillage the Peugeot pansies!! I want the first born of every single-occupant vehicle!!
©Phil (HABEAS CORRUPTUS) Frank
You can't do that, sir... ..it's illegal.
Oh, how I long for the good old days..

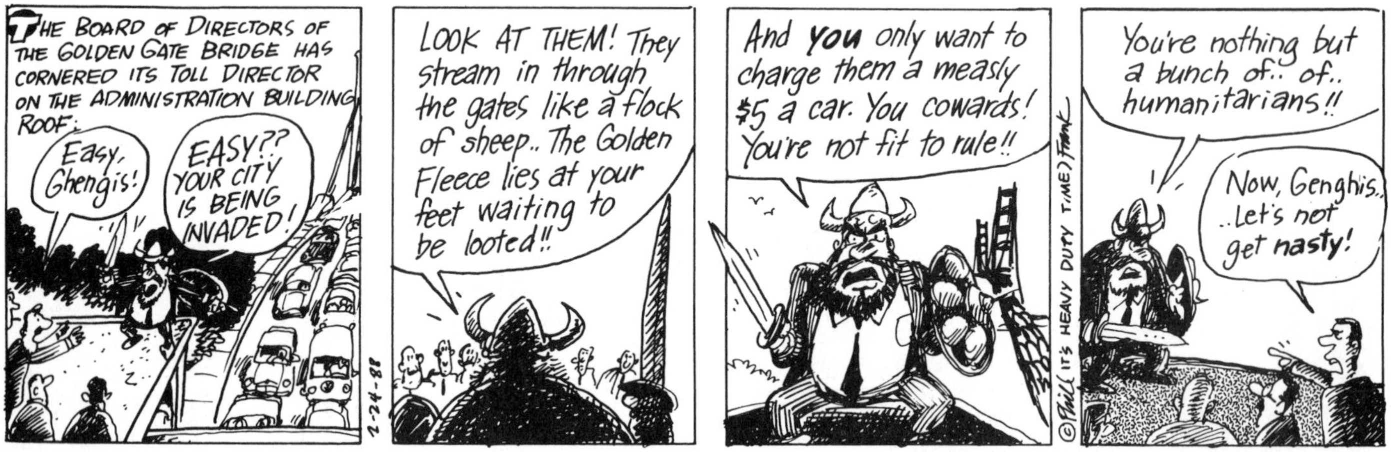
THE BOARD OF DIRECTORS OF THE GOLDEN GATE BRIDGE HAS CORNERED ITS TOLL DIRECTOR ON THE ADMINISTRATION BUILDING ROOF:
Easy, Ghengis!
EASY?? YOUR CITY IS BEING INVADED!
2-24-88
LOOK AT THEM! They stream in through the gates like a flock of sheep.. The Golden Fleece lies at your feet waiting to be looted!!
And **you** only want to charge them a measly $5 a car. You cowards! You're not fit to rule!!
©Phil (IT'S HEAVY DUTY TIME) Frank
You're nothing but a bunch of.. of.. humanitarians!!
Now, Genghis.. ..Let's not get **nasty**!

AT THE TOP OF THE SOUTH TOWER OF THE GOLDEN GATE BRIDGE, **G. GORDON KHAN**, BRIDGE TOLL DIRECTOR, SEEKS A SIGN FROM THE GODS:

Oh, spirits of the sky and water..

How do I solve the bridge toll crisis? Give me a sign...

Fuji

Fuji?

What does this mean.. ..an invasion from the East?

AHA!! NOW I SEE! Make the commuter hordes pay their tolls in **yen**!

© Phill (FILM AT ELEVEN) Frank

THE GOLDEN GATE BRIDGE BOARD MEETS IN CLOSED-DOOR SESSION:

HEY! THAT WAS A GREAT TACTIC! THREATEN TO RAISE THE TOLL TO FIVE DOLLARS!!

YEAH, THEN ONLY RAISE IT TO TWO AND COMMUTERS THINK THEY GOT OFF EASY!!

HAW!! HAW!!

G. GORDON KHAN, STAFF MEMBER, MAKES HIS MOVE:

Before we raise the toll to two dollars I think we should make them pay in **other** ways..

How, Genghis?

Emotionally..!! I love to watch those commuters squirm!!

© PHIL MISSOURI LOVES COMPANY Frank

Okay, tolltakers.. all together.. after me..

"Good Morning! You can go into the city today but you can't come back."

"Good Morning.. you can go.."

G. GORDON KHAN, GOLDEN GATE BRIDGE DISTRICT STAFF MEMBER, SURVEYS THE SCENE:

Hee..Hee.. Hee.. Look at those hordes of commuters.

My little lemmings..! **Each** with **two** dollars for my coffers! Come to me, my little lambs!

NEXT YEAR I'LL WANT YOUR FIRSTBORN!

© Phil CASK NOT FOR WHOM THE BRIDGE TOLLS) Frank

Ooooooooo... .. I just **LOVE** TOLL INCREASES!!

"The wife killed the inspector."

I decided, a year before the strip went local, that Farley needed a foil. I wanted a pet but an independent one that would come and go. Ravens had always fascinated me so I created Bruce. For the first year of his existence, he was rather poorly drawn. Luckily I obtained a stuffed raven as a model and his appearance improved noticeably. Bruce moved easily into the city's avian world.

"Oh. I see it's time for you humans to revel in your barbaric feast again."

"Look, Bruce. We've been through this before. A turkey is not like a raven. It's a domesticated animal."

"Hmmph!"

"Besides.. I'm celebrating Thanksgiving at Irene's. She's cooking the bird. All I'm preparing is the pumpkin pie."

"Pumpkin?"

"You eat poor defenseless pumpkins, too?"

©Phil (YOU EAT WHAT YOU ARE) Frank

"Hey, Bruce.. what're you doing?"

"Looking at the personal effects of your Thanksgiving turkey.."

"His graduation photograph.. ..his comb... ..his social security card.."

"Stop trying to lay a guilt trip on me about having turkey for Thanks..."

"Please, Farley.. I'm in mourning. Could you mail his things?"

©Phil (A LIFE IS A TERRIBLE THING TO BASTE) Frank

"He had a family in Turlock?"

A SCRATCHING AND SQUEAKING IN THE WALLS ROUSES BRUCE FROM HIS TORPOR.

SQUEAK!! SQUEAK!!

Farley!! Bad news. We've got mice.

I know. I baited a trap last night..

3-27-89

This Brie is a cheap domestic.. ..barely aged..

How gauche!

SNIFF! SNIFF!

Worse news. We've got yuppie mice.

©Phil (MICE-A-RONI) Frank

THE NEWS THAT A FAMILY OF YUPPIE MICE HAS MOVED INTO HIS WALL HAS FARLEY IN A DITHER:

YUPPIE MICE?

THEY'RE IMPOSSIBLE TO GET RID OF!!

SQUEAK! SQUEAK!

IT WOULD APPEAR THAT THERE IS TENSION IN THE RODENT RANKS AS WELL.

I wanted to move into a nice upscale neighborhood like the Haight..

3-30-89

But you... you pick a run-down flat in North Beach with a low-brow bachelor who can't buy a well-aged cheese or a decent Chablis!!

©Phil (HIT THE ROADENT) Frank

And where, in this hole-in-the-wall, is our au pair to live, pray tell?

Psst! You may not have to get rid of them. They may move!

AN AVIAN PARTY IS UNDER WAY AT A NORTH BEACH FLAT:

So... Bruce lives here with a bachelor, eh? I like the earth tones...

That's dirt.

Please.. no more quail jokes.

Yeah.. It's great when the kids are finally out of the nest..

I know this little bar with free munchies.

Cheep! Cheep! Cheep!

Sorry, pal. No pigeons.

Love the 'do. Where'd you have it done?

SOMA.

Jeesh! Leave it to a seagull to stand in the hors d'oeuvres.

Nice party, Bruce.

8-10-89

THE FEATHER REPORT

Urban Pet Quiz: What one item, more than any other, has helped nature maintain the order of the species?

12-17-88

NUDGE!

EEEEEEEE

The Exocat Missile, of course.

(© PHIL BEANIES FROM HEAVEN) Frank

CRASH!

Why should **you** know how my new answering machine works?

Just curious.

Well.. this little light means there's a message so I push this button to hear it.

Hey, Bruce,.. baby!! It's Blackie, your wingman..

1-28-89

Met two Bohemian Waxwings of the female persuasion over Angel Island this morning.. They're new in the area...

(© PHIL CIAO DOWN.) Frank

We're gonna meet at 1400 hours over Coit Tower to hit the Pyracantha berries on the north slope of Telegraph. Be there or be square. Ciao!

Thanks! I'm outta here.

BAY AREA BIRDWATCHERS HAVE EXPERIENCED A RECENT WINDFALL OF RARE BIRD SIGHTINGS DURING THE SAN FRANCISCO BIRD COUNT:

A Yellow-headed blackbird!!

LOOK!! A RUFOUS-CROWNED SPARROW!

1-9-88

WOW!.. A TROPICAL KINGBIRD!

GOOD LORD!! WHAT DO YOU MAKE OF **THIS** ONE?

(© PHIL TOUCAN PLAY THIS GAME.) Frank

I love toying with birdwatchers' minds..

Bruce... did you know that the history of the raven goes all the way back to Noah's ark..

Really?

3-19-90

Apparently, Noah first released a raven to find land and only when it didn't return did Noah release the dove.

Gee, what happened to the poor raven?

I could guess.

?

© PAUL (DOUBLE OCCUPANCY REQUIRED) FRANK

Oh, man.. Is it ever great to be off that boat..

BRUCE HAS FLOWN DOWN SOUTH FOR THE WEEKEND TO THE POSH SEASHORE TOWN OF HUNTINGTON BEACH:

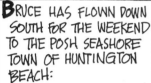

Hmm..

What a mess.. There's crude oil everywhere..

3-2-90

GOTCHA!

© PAUL (THE OILY BIRD GETS THE WORKS) FRANK

Get that detergent bath ready!

I got an oil-soaked seagull!

I think I should've gone to Fresno..

Come on, Bruce. Get into the spirit of it. It's Halloween. Let's switch roles..

Do I make a great raven or what?

I'm speechless.

10-31

Put on your outfit. Come on!

All Right! All Right!

© PAUL (THE MANBIRD OF ALCATRAZ) FRANK

This is, like, really weird.

What **is** this thing about the anniversary of Woodstock? I don't get it.

8-16-89

The Age of Aquarius.. peace, love, brotherhood. What was the big deal?

What about you? **You'd** know if anyone would.

Woodstock says you had to be there to understand..

©Full FARM OUT!!! Frank

I'D RATHER BE HIBERNATING

Fall and a chill is in the air. Baseball season has given way to football and the bears, heavy with salmon, take to their den beneath the FOG CITY DUMPSTER for hibernation. Above ground, wars are fought, traffic drones, horns blow, the Dow-Jones rises and falls and life hurtles along at an ungodly pace. Occasionally we peek in at our furry foursome, snug in their dark cozy bedroom, dreaming of honey pots and we are very very jealous.

ALPHONSE PREPARES TO HIBERNATE:

I'm feeling pretty sleepy.. I think I'll call it a year..

Been a tough one for you, with the Giants and all..

11-14-89

Very old are we bears, Our dreams are tales Told in dim lairs By eve's nightingales;

We wake and whisper awhile. But the day gone by...

©Full NO REST FOR THE WHIPPET Frank

Silence and sleep like fields Of flowers lie..

To my bower do I now retire..

I thought you already went off to hibernate, Alphonse.

I fear that sleep's calm mantle will not lie soothingly upon my shoulders..

Look.. we know you're upset by the Giants vote..

But **maybe** while you're taking a long hibernation, Mayor Agnos will figure out a way for the Giants to stay in San Francisco..

Really, Hilda?

To sleep.. ..perchance to dream..

I'll be in in a week or so..

For three months the bears are asleep, gone from the strip, and then....

HILDA IS THE FIRST TO RISE FROM HIBERNATION. SHE IS GREETED BY FOUR MONTHS OF **CHRONICLES**:

CITY DUMPST

WHY NOT WORRY?

WORLD NEWS UPDATE!! BERLIN WALL DOWN! EAST AND WEST GERMANY TO UNIFY!! MANDELA OUT OF PRISON!

ROMANIA THROWS OFF SHACKLES OF COMMUNISM!?!. ORTEGA OUSTED IN NICARAGUAN VOTE!! LITHUANIANS DECLARE INDEPENDENCE!! SOVIET BLOC IN DISARRAY!

WHILE DOWN IN THE DEN, ALPHONSE'S MIND IS ON OTHER THINGS:

Three pounds of Gummi Bears and a six-pack of Twinkies, please..

NOW FOR THE LOCAL NEWS.

NEXT TO AWAKEN FROM WINTER HIBERNATION IS *Franklin D. (Roosevelt) Bear*

YAWN

..THE "ENFANT TERRIBLE" OF THE CLAN, HE RISES AND STRAPS ON HIS BANDOLEROS..

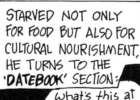

STARVED NOT ONLY FOR FOOD BUT ALSO FOR CULTURAL NOURISHMENT, HE TURNS TO THE 'DATEBOOK' SECTION:

What's this at the Marines' Memorial Theater?

"I DON'T HAVE TO SHOW YOU NO STINKING BADGES" by Luis Valdez..

I'm outta here!!

HEY! What about your breakfast?

IRENE THE METERMAID: The paper had done a series of stories about the lives of Parking Control Officers (Meter Maids). I thought it an interesting challenge to create a sympathetic following for someone in such a thankless job. Irene's a single mother of a precocious daughter (Olive). Her career on the streets of the city has hardened her a bit. The parking officers slip me ideas and have given Irene her own radio call letters. Notice how her facial features change as her character develops.

MR. FARLEY!! I am Emma Nusbaum from Pinole and I for one am sick and tired of being strung along!

Wha.

You know what I mean!! You and that meter maid, Irene. When are you two going to get it on? It's Valentine's Day. Call Her!!

But, I.

Hi, Irene.. Farley here.. ..just called to wish you a happy Valentine's day..

Let's get together..

I'd love to, Farley.. when?

UH..AS SOON AS POSSIBLE.

Farley is being forced by an irate reader from Pinole to pursue his relationship with the metermaid.

This is her apartment..

Ring the bell.. and no funny stuff..

Hi, Farley.. Ohh.. Flowers!!

..and candy..

..and Mrs. Nusbaum..

?

She has a question to ask you..

Do you, Irene, take this man to be your lawfully..

Please, Mrs. Nusbaum.. I appreciate your concern for my relationship with Irene, but..

No BUTS about it! When are you going to ask her?

Why are you so anxious to see me married?

Well.. to be quite frank..

My "Two-For-One" subscription offer runs out in a week. I'll never know the outcome.. Please!. ..for an old lady..

You can help.. or you can turn the page.

Or I can renew her subscription.

IT'S TRAFFIC AWARENESS WEEK:

What are you doing, officer?

I'm writing this Volvo a ticket.

5-27

But.. that's **my** car, and it has commercial plates..

and it's been here over an hour **and** it's not being used for a commercial pickup.

Ohh.. but officer, I'm late for the matinee..

Ahh.. the matinee.. Delightful.

Uhh. **no**.. I'm late for the **mat..in..a**.. uh.. bedding store. I run a judo school and I need a new mat..

Have a nice day.

© PhiL Life ain't no "Cabaret" Frank

O Henry 98! Calling O Henry 98! This is dispatch. Over.

O Henry 98 here. Over.

I'm patching through a call for you. Over.

Hello? Irene?

Farley? I told you not to call me at work!

8-23-88

I'm sorry but I need to talk to you. Where can we meet?

I'm going on break in five minutes. I'm on Ellis Street..

I'm at the 1976 blue Subaru station wagon. It has a "Ducks Unlimited" bumper sticker and a bent coat hanger for an aerial..

This is the weirdest relationship..

© PhiL PARKING IS SUCH SWEET SORROW Frank

THE METER MAID AND THE REPORTER CONSOLE EACH OTHER..

So commuting from San Jose was rough..

The things I do for a story..

I feel the same way about ticketing cars all day.

This really **is** becoming an automobile society.

6-13

And we're trapped in it! Slaves to the very vehicles intended to give us freedom.

I know **exactly** what you mean!

Farley... we need to develop other common interests...

Besides Bay Area road conditions?

© PhiL AUTO EROTICA Frank

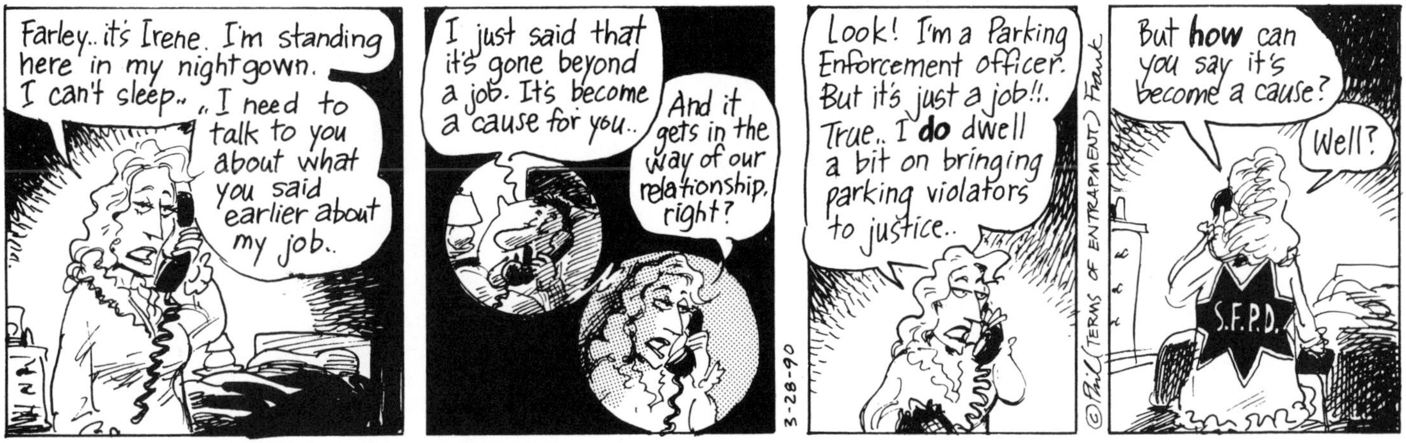

Farley.. it's Irene. I'm standing here in my nightgown. I can't sleep..
.. I need to talk to you about what you said earlier about my job..
I just said that it's gone beyond a job. It's become a cause for you..
And it gets in the way of our relationship, right?
3-28-90
Look! I'm a Parking Enforcement officer. But it's just a job!!. True.. I **do** dwell a bit on bringing parking violators to justice..
© Phil (TERMS OF ENTRAPMENT) Frank
But **how** can you say it's become a cause?
Well?
S.F.P.D.

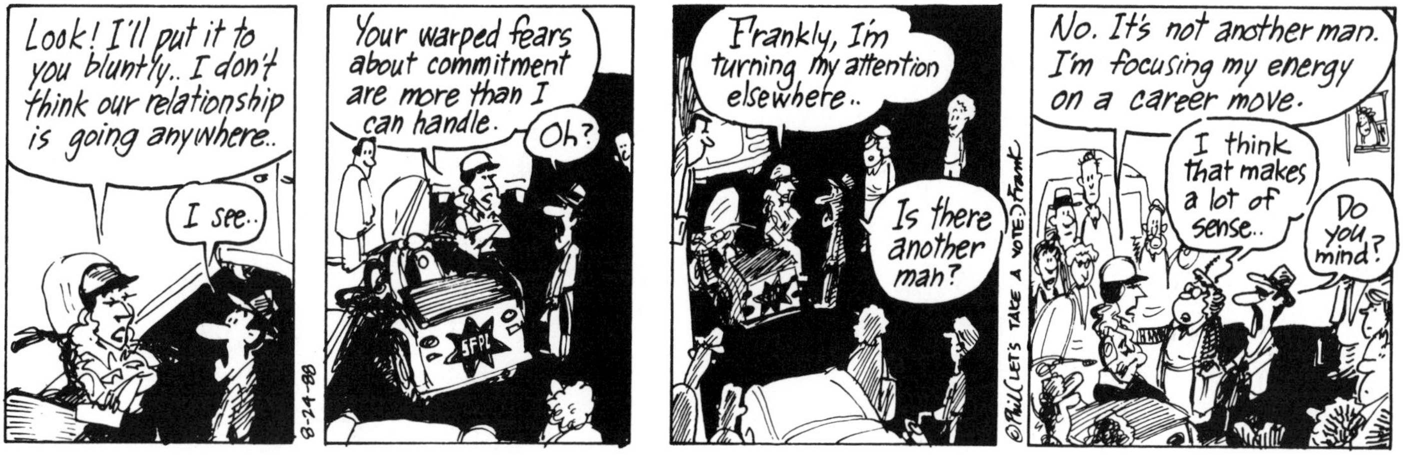

Look! I'll put it to you bluntly.. I don't think our relationship is going anywhere..
I see..
8-24-88
Your warped fears about commitment are more than I can handle.
Oh?
SFPD
Frankly, I'm turning my attention elsewhere..
Is there another man?
© Phil (LET'S TAKE A VOTE.) Frank
No. It's not another man. I'm focusing my energy on a career move.
I think that makes a lot of sense..
Do you mind?

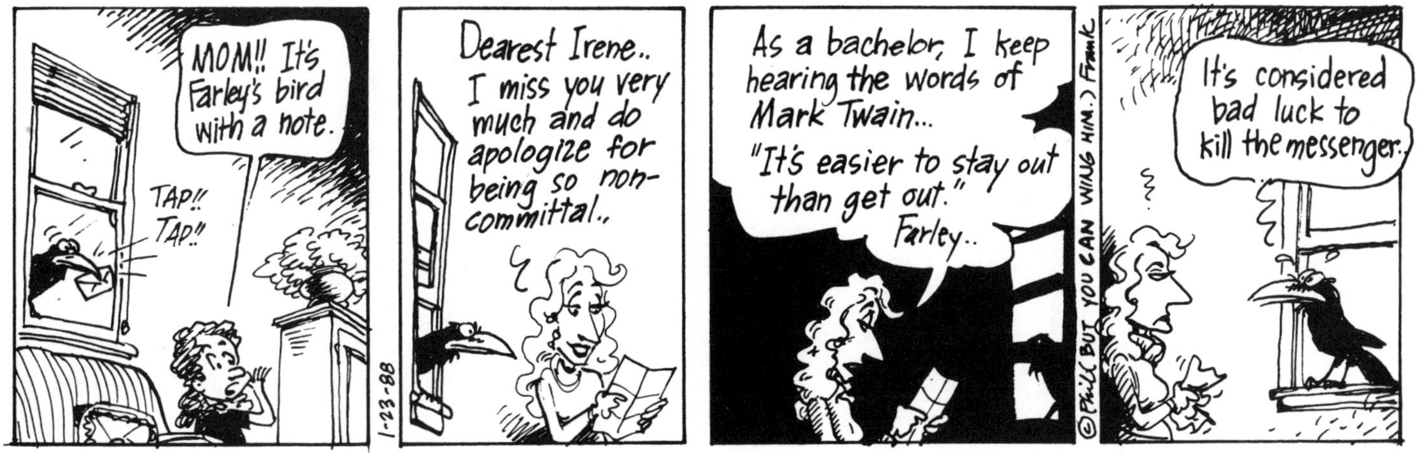

MOM!! It's Farley's bird with a note.
TAP!! TAP!!
1-23-88
Dearest Irene.. I miss you very much and do apologize for being so non-committal..
As a bachelor, I keep hearing the words of Mark Twain... "It's easier to stay out than get out." Farley..
© Phil (BUT YOU CAN WING HIM.) Frank
It's considered bad luck to kill the messenger.

Farley's girlfriend, the meter maid, put a "Las Vegas boot" on him. She won't unlock it until he makes a marriage commitment..

Really?

Have you heard about Farley and his girlfriend, the meter maid? She gave him some boots from Las Vegas as a marriage gift..

Oh?

Listen.. I'm not one to spread gossip, but Farley's girlfriend has given him the boot. Apparently there was a meter maid in Las Vegas involved..

No!.

You CAD!

?

© Phil (NOT THE VEGAS IDEA..) Frank

11-28-89

BY SECURING A ROLLER SKATE TO THE BOTTOM OF HIS "LAS VEGAS BOOT" FARLEY HAS ATTAINED A SENSE OF MOBILITY:

I'd kneel, Baba, but I couldn't get up again..

What has driven your ladyfriend to this?

FAX BABA 332-9197

DANGER BAD PUN AHEAD

11-29-89

Marriage!! She wants a commitment from me or she won't unlock it!!

Clearly a desperate woman! Here's some advice for her..

HIT IT!

YOU CAN'T ALWAYS GET WHAT YOU WAAAANNT!..♪ No.. YOU CAN'T ALWAYS GET WHAT YOU WANT...

© Phil (BAD PUN A'RISIN..) Frank

What was THAT?

My Baba shop quartet.

That'll be $50.

AT THE BLACKSMITH SHOP ON BRANNAN STREET FARLEY HAS THE "LAS VEGAS BOOT" REMOVED.

You know, technically it's against the 'law for me to cut this thing off..

CLANG! CLANG!

BLACKSMITH

At least once a week I get some guy in here whose ladyfriend has put one of these on him..

CLANG!!!

12-4-89

When a woman resorts to a device like this, it's her way of showing you how shackled she feels by the relationship..

© Phil (TRY TO IRON THINGS OUT..) Frank

Great.. blacksmith as therapist.. yet another California experience..

The key is learning to share your feelings..

CLANG!

Farley.. It's Irene... I know I wasn't going to call you again.. but I am **so** angry...

2-10-88

I have **got** to get these things off my chest! First of all..

COUGH! COUGH!

What's wrong with you? Why are you coughing?

The flu? What are you taking for it? **Diet Coke?** Have you eaten anything? **Pizza?**

Listen.. I'm bringing you some dinner and fresh fruit later. Bye.

Drat! Mother Teresa wins out over Joan Crawford once again...

© Phil (THE FEMININE MYSTAQUE) Frank

IRENE, OUR LOVELY METERMAID, POURS OUT HER SOUL TO HER CONFIDANTE AND SINGLES SCENE ADVISOR, FERN BARRE:

I'm so tired of waiting for Farley to make a commitment..

4-15-88

You need to stir the soup, honey. Circulate.. ..date other men.. Send Farley a strong signal!

But, Fern... how can a respectable single mother meet men easily?

Here. Give this woman a call..

"Mrs. Stark's Reality Dating Service"?

Here.. You can even use my Frequent Dater card..

© Phil (HERDED THROUGH THE GRAPEVINE) Frank

IN AN ATTEMPT TO MAKE OR BREAK HER RELATIONSHIP WITH FARLEY, IRENE VISITS A DATING SERVICE:

STARK'S REALITY DATING SERVICE

I demand from my clients a certain amount of reality..

4-16-88

I don't supply Supermen or other Hollywood-type fantasies.. I help **real** people get together.

That sounds reasonable..

Okay.. let's get started..

Well... I've pared my requirements down to three things..

My date should have a job, not be married and not be a psychopath.

(SIGH!) You newcomers sure are picky..

© Phil (THE LAW OF BELOW-AVERAGES) Frank

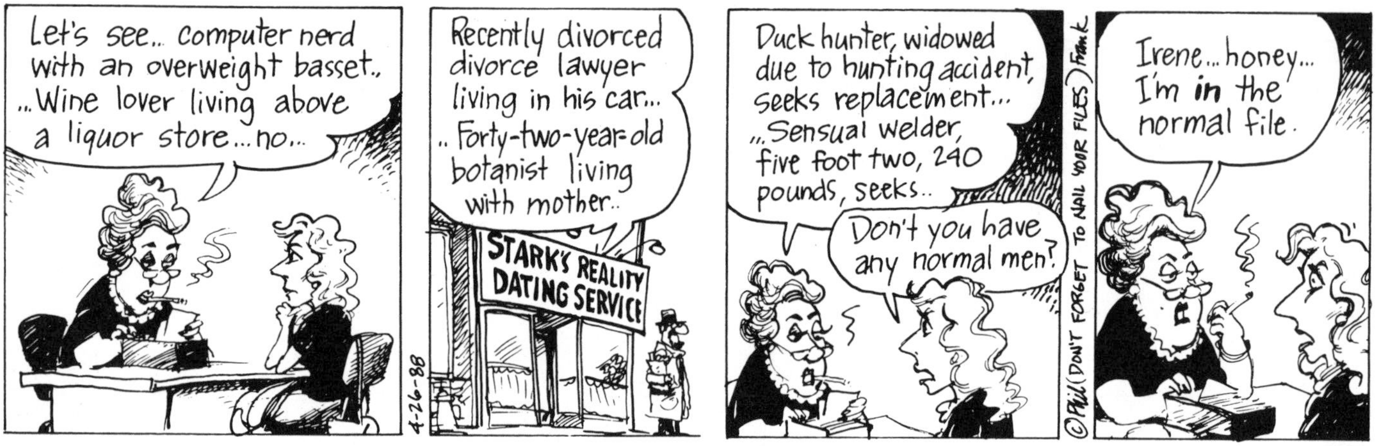
Let's see... computer nerd with an overweight basset.. ...Wine lover living above a liquor store...no...
4-26-88
Recently divorced divorce lawyer living in his car... .. Forty-two-year-old botanist living with mother..
STARK'S REALITY DATING SERVICE
Duck hunter, widowed due to hunting accident, seeks replacement... ...Sensual welder, five foot two, 240 pounds, seeks..
Don't you have any normal men?
©Phil (DON'T FORGET TO NAIL YOUR FILES) Frank
Irene... honey... I'm **in** the normal file.

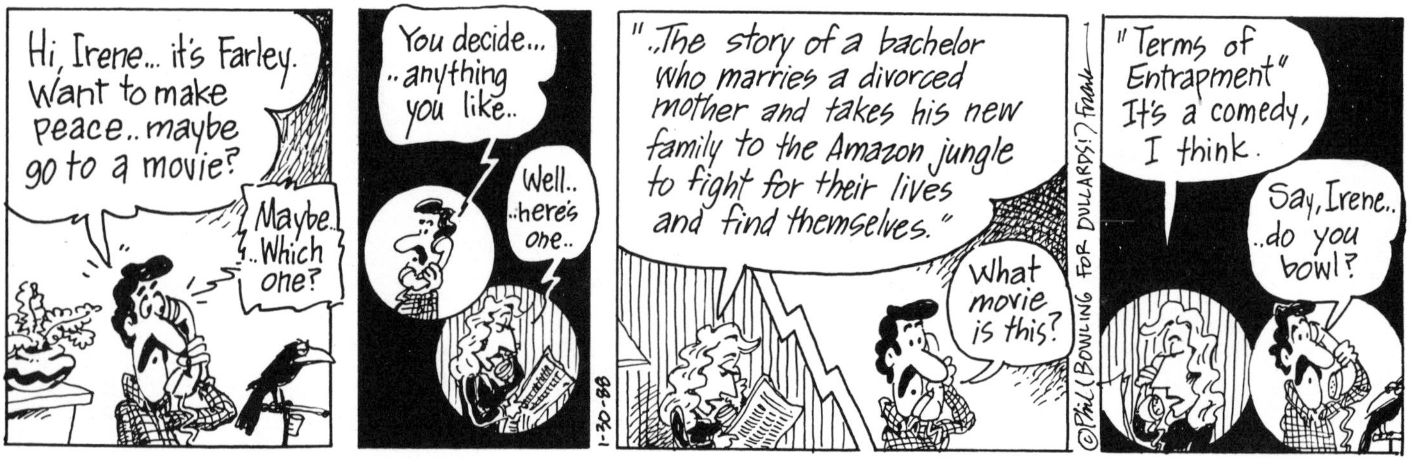
Hi, Irene... it's Farley. Want to make peace.. maybe go to a movie?
Maybe.. ..Which one?
You decide... ..anything you like..
Well.. ..here's one..
1-30-88
"..The story of a bachelor who marries a divorced mother and takes his new family to the Amazon jungle to fight for their lives and find themselves."
What movie is this?
©Phil (BOWLING FOR DULLARDS!) Frank
"Terms of Entrapment" It's a comedy, I think.
Say, Irene.. ..do you bowl?

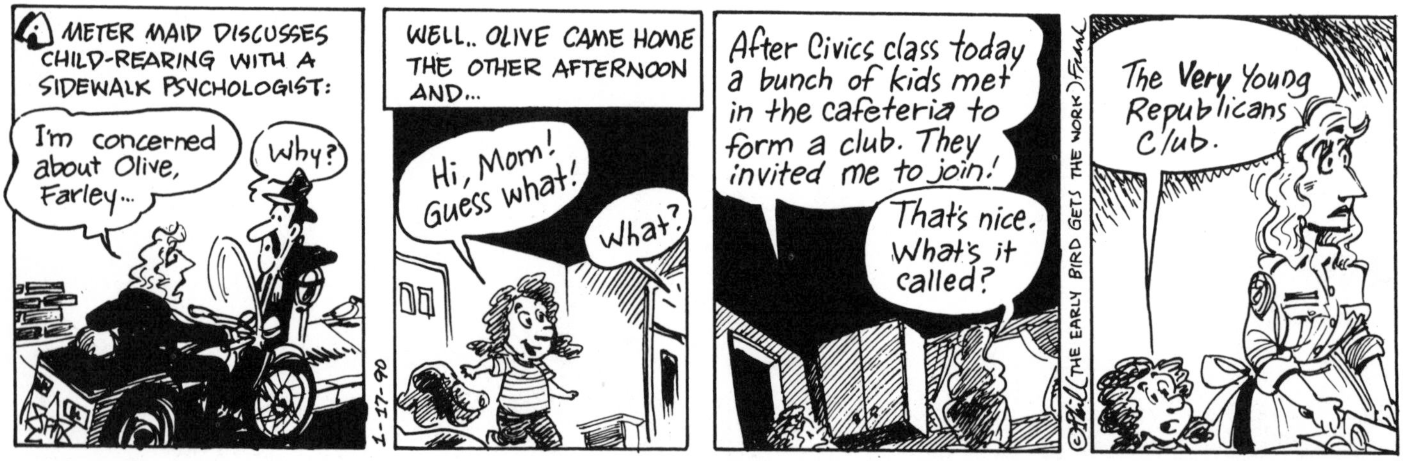
METER MAID DISCUSSES CHILD-REARING WITH A SIDEWALK PSYCHOLOGIST:
I'm concerned about Olive, Farley...
Why?
1-17-90
WELL.. OLIVE CAME HOME THE OTHER AFTERNOON AND...
Hi, Mom! Guess what!
What?
After Civics class today a bunch of kids met in the cafeteria to form a club. They invited me to join!
That's nice. What's it called?
©Phil (THE EARLY BIRD GETS THE WORK) Frank
The **Very** Young Republicans Club.

THE NEW YEAR FINDS SOME OLD QUESTIONS UNANSWERED..

Well, I don't think a little commitment is too much to ask..

1-2-88

After all.. we've been dating for two years, we're not seeing anyone else... and.. and...

..and what?

..old

© Paul Miss Quote, 1988) Frank

And on one occasion I even heard Olive call you "Dad"..

THAT WAS STRICTLY OFF THE RECORD!!

FARLEY AND IRENE DINE OUT:

Look, Irene... I'm serious. I am making some very big changes in my life..

Uh huh.

There is a new man emerging from within me!

Tell me about him. What's he like?

10-4-89

Well, he's no wimp! He's assertive, knows who he is and isn't afraid to stand up and say it!

There's one thing I'd like to know about this new guy. Does he have...

A POTBELLY? DO I HAVE A POTBELLY??

© Paul Living beyond my seams) Frank

IN A LONG-STANDING TRADITION (THREE YEARS), A PAIR OF LOVEBIRDS GREET THE NEW YEAR FROM COIT TOWER:

Sun's up, Irene..

Unhh..

1-1-90

I was just thinking about how different our lives would've been if I hadn't given you a ticket that New Year's Eve..

Ah, yes..

We'd never have met, gotten entrenched in each other's psyches, squabbled, made up, sought professional counseling and maxxed out our credit cards on a weekend in Carmel!

© Paul I ink, therefore I am) Frank

You should be more careful about who you give tickets to..

That's one of my New Year's resolutions..

Homelessness is a tough but everpresent issue.. especially in San Francisco where the climate and services available have drawn an increasing number of the destitute. I brought in a character from the syndicated strip... Beppo. He's a sensitive, down-on-his-luck Vietnam vet who lives in an abandoned Gremlin and is available as a sounding board for any news related to homeless issues.

Ahh.. Smell that air, Farley.. the fragrance of autumn. I love the City in the early fall...

Behold nature's paint-brush at work... the rich reds and golds and the lush greens..

The sounds of the City's migratory visitors flocking south..

HONK
HONK

HONK!

9-26-87

Beppo.. is your poetic license current?

Sad to say it was revoked for Rhyming Under the Influence..

©Phil (DON'T DRINK AND RHYME) Frank

Have you seen the comics today, Beppo? Lots of 'em are about the homeless..

Oh?

10-25-88

Seems that our cartoonists are using their wit-tipped lances to lampoon the powers that be for ignoring the plight of the less fortunate.

Well said!

Finally we're getting some coverage.

Aw, that's nothin' new..

Newspapers been coverin' the homeless for years...

©Phil LET'S FACE THE FACTS) Frank

A Man-In-The-Street interview? The question, Beppo, is: "How do you feel about tourists?"

Oh! I find our visitors to be pretty decent. Definitely better tippers than the locals. And they're especially generous...

..when I do my noontime "Dance of Death" crossing against the light at Sixth and Market. Dance.. ..of.. Death..

© Phil (DANCING CHEEK TO JOWL) Frank   1-17

Present weather conditions explained!.. 25¢! Long-range forecasts... 50¢! Present conditions.

A high-pressure system over Nevada, created by a clear ridge in the jet stream, is pushing all storms northward.

1-31

This causes clear skies in the Bay Area at night and loss of ground heat.

How does a street person know so much about the weather? Hey, man. We're specialists!

© Phil (VIRUS CON DIOS) Frank

Beppo... What do you know about these bogus "Scenic Drive" signs on an alley off Sixth and Mission?

NAT   49 MILE SCENIC DRIVE

1-16

Bogus? Is this not **scenic**? Is this not fraught with wildlife?

Are these not towering redwood crates? Are these not part of our beautiful bay's bounty?

Beppo! It wasn't meant to be a "Scenic By-Product Route." Says who?

© Phil (MERE WOODS) Frank

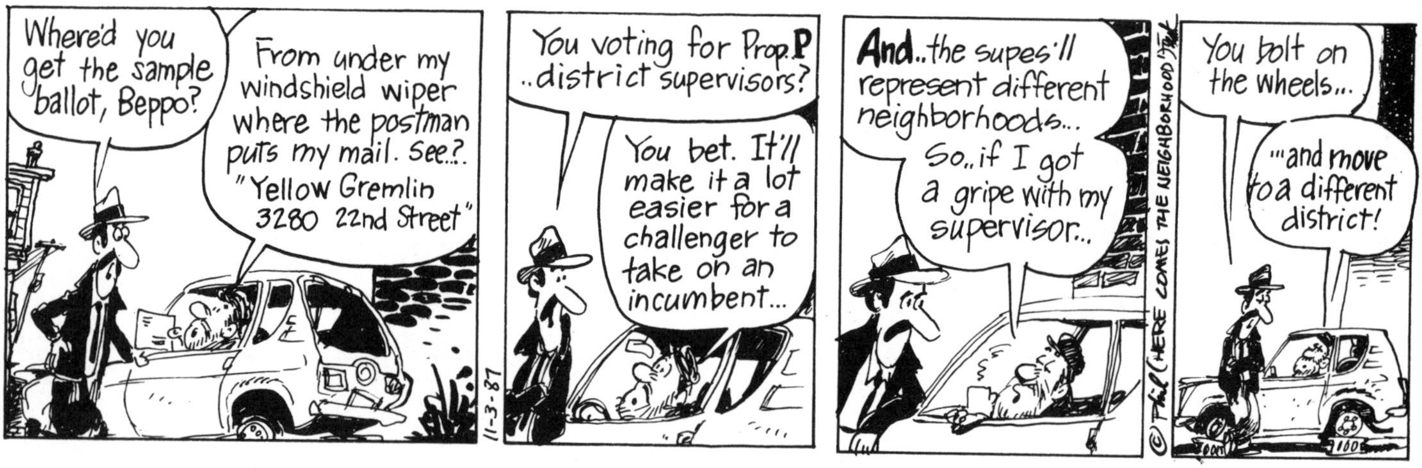
Where'd you get the sample ballot, Beppo?
From under my windshield wiper where the postman puts my mail. See?.. "Yellow Gremlin 3280 22nd Street"
11-3-87
You voting for Prop. P ..district supervisors?
You bet. It'll make it a lot easier for a challenger to take on an incumbent...
And..the supes'll represent different neighborhoods...
So..if I got a gripe with my supervisor...
© Phil Frank (HERE COMES THE NEIGHBORHOOD)
You bolt on the wheels...
...and move to a different district!

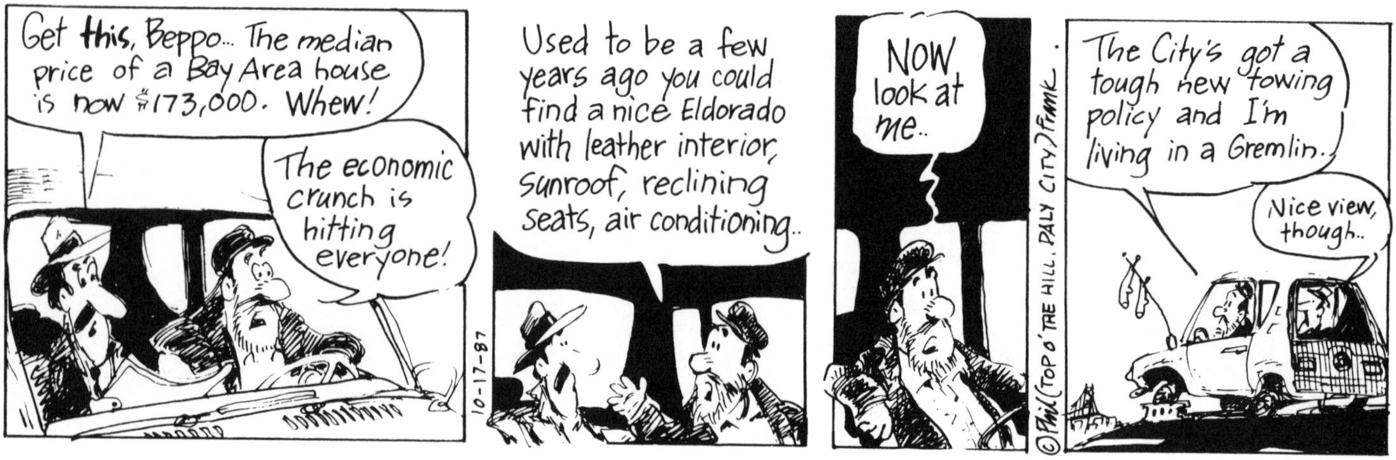
Get this, Beppo... The median price of a Bay Area house is now $173,000. Whew!
The economic crunch is hitting everyone!
10-17-87
Used to be a few years ago you could find a nice Eldorado with leather interior, sunroof, reclining seats, air conditioning..
NOW look at me..
© Phil Frank (TOP O' THE HILL, DALY CITY)
The City's got a tough new towing policy and I'm living in a Gremlin..
Nice view, though..

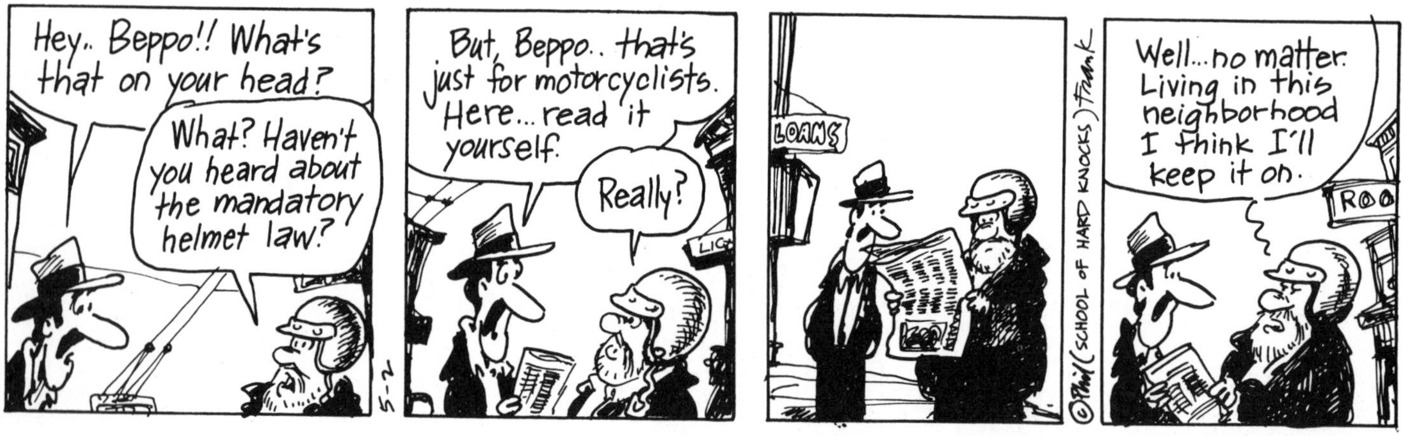
Hey.. Beppo!! What's that on your head?
What? Haven't you heard about the mandatory helmet law?
5-2
But, Beppo.. that's just for motorcyclists. Here... read it yourself.
Really?
LOANS
© Phil Frank (SCHOOL OF HARD KNOCKS)
Well... no matter. Living in this neighborhood I think I'll keep it on.

Jeez, this is great to get out in the woods and away from the street life, Beppo..

It's very peaceful..

1-16-90

The wind whistling through the evergreens..

No cars.. ..no concrete, ..no noise. Nature abounds..

Beppo!! Look! A birdie! I see a birdie!

That's a pigeon!

A pigeon? There aren't pigeons in the woods!

So true.

© Phil (Tree's company.) Frank

What's **with** you reporters? All those biased stories about abandoned cars..

But, Beppo..

2-21

Think of what a nuisance these abandoned cars are to the neighborhood..

NUISANCE? But, Farley... ..you're talking about choice rolling rental units.

© Phil (Midnight Rambler.) Frank

Blocking sidewalks.. ..inhibiting parking..

HEY! CAPED CRUSADER!! Knock it off! People are trying to sleep!

You stay out of this. You're 2 months behind in your rent.

These abandoned vehicles, which **you** view as a blight on the neighborhoods...

..."I happen to view as an asset..cheap housing.. and an opportunity for the small businessman..

ROOM FOR RENT

2-22

BUT BEPPO!! THERE ARE OVER **700** OLD CARS CLOGGING THE CITY STREETS..

Seven hundred? Gee.. I guess I should think this out more.

© Phil (The greatest story ever towed.) Frank

They're public eyesores.. Hazards to the common..

700 cars.. at $75 minimum a month... ..$125 near the Marina..

BEEP BEEP BEEP.

FARLEY'S FACT FILE..
SOME THINGS YOU NEVER KNEW ABOUT SAN FRANCISCO'S HOMELESS..

ACCORDING TO SOME CITY OFFICIALS: THE CITY'S HOMELESS ARE THERE BECAUSE THEY **WANT** TO BE.

You coming to the shelter? It's freezing out here.

Not me. I love the sound of the rain.

..INCREASED AID WILL ENCOURAGE FREELOADERS FROM OTHER CITIES...

I can't decide, Alice.. Should we go to Mexico or hang out in the streets of San Francisco?

..SOME PEOPLE USE FAKE IDENTITIES TO GET INCREASED BENEFITS.

Jerry Brown? I thought you were in Japan.

Oh! uh.. I came back to be with my people.

THE MAYOR'S COMMITTEE ON THE HOMELESS CONSIDERS YET ANOTHER POSSIBLE SOLUTION.

Here's a concept that could solve **both** the housing **and** feeding simultaneously!

Edible housing! ..Structures built of nutritious algae bricks!

They're great with a little A-1 Sauce.

AND...if, after a couple of years, they're homeless again, they'll have only **themselves** to blame!!

FARLEY CONTINUES TO RESEARCH HIS STORY ON THE CITY'S HOMELESS..

What are **your** plans, Glenda?

Well, with this dark mood of civic distrust of us street folks, I'm thinkin' of a change of climate soon.

I've heard Tahoe is beautiful in the fall..

What's holding you back?

You ever tried to get snow tires for a shopping cart?

VISITOR ARRIVES AT THE CITY ROOM OF THE DAILY REQUIREMENT.

Hey, Beppo! You're looking dapper.

8-12

My card.

Oh?

Beppo. Public Relations Consultant representing the displaced, downtrodden and undernourished citizenry of San Francisco.

My lunch.

Care for a wedge of surplus cheese?

© Phil (I TILSIT LIKE IT IS) Frank

You've got your finger on the City's pulse, Farley. Tell me what our malady is..

What're the symptoms?

SOFT PRETZELS

8-13

A few bad apples are making it rough for all us street people..

Most of us are good people down on our luck. Now the press kicks us too. It's like we have a disease..

You do, Beppo.

© Phil (FILM AT ELEVEN) Frank

You have the worst affliction any group that wants to survive the 80's could have. You have an image problem!

My worst fears realized!!

BEPPO GIVES FARLEY THE PITCH..

These people are not a tax on our system. They're making it on their own!

8-14

They're out there in the urban wilderness, braving the elements, lack of supplies, inhospitable surroundings.. attacks from hostiles.

© Phil (CIRCLE YOUR SHOPPING CART) Frank

These street people are the pioneers of the 1980's!!

You have a future in public relations, Beppo. I think the Golden Gate Bridge District could use someone like you.

BEPPO, SELF-APPOINTED PUBLIC RELATIONS REP FOR THE CITY'S HOMELESS, SHARES SOME THOUGHTS WITH THE REPORTER.

They may be homeless but they're not helpless.

8-15-90

But Beppo...do you think these people are capable of taking care of themselves?

WHAT?

Who has more sense? Glenda with her twelve layers of sweaters,

..Or that family of tourists freezing in their T-shirts?

Got a point there.

© Phil (SPARE CHANGE OF CLOTHES?) Frank

What I don't understand, Beppo... is why the Mayor can't come up with a simple, clear solution to the homeless issue..

1-9-90

Excuse me, folks...what do you think the City should do about the homeless?

The City **must** reach out with compassion and care and do everything possible.

The City should round 'em up, put 'em all in train cars and ship 'em to Nevada!

Well?

© Phil TAKE THE "H" TRAIN) Frank

Well, Beppo... my best wishes go with you. You've picked a thankless job... being the public relations person for the homeless..

1-10-90

Thanks for coming, Farley..!! Any favorable comments in the press would be appreciated.

I'll see what I can do.

© Phil (PICKY, PICKY, PICKY...) Frank

Hey, Beppo..!! Keep reminding your constituents.. ..Some of the best things in life are free..!!

Unfortunately, so are some of the worst!

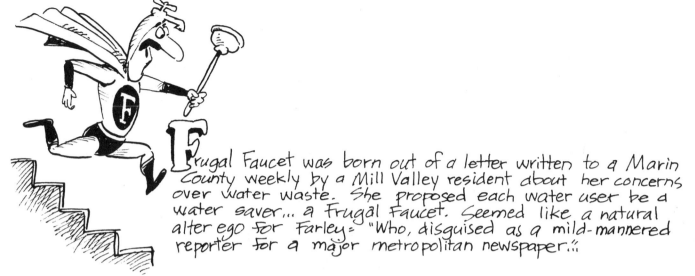

Frugal Faucet was born out of a letter written to a Marin County weekly by a Mill Valley resident about her concerns over water waste. She proposed each water user be a water saver... a Frugal Faucet. Seemed like a natural alter ego for Farley: "Who, disguised as a mild-mannered reporter for a major metropolitan newspaper..."

THE TENSION LEVEL RISES DRAMATICALLY AS THE LATEST FIGURES ON THE SNOW PACK ARE RECEIVED AT THE WATER DEPARTMENT:

Hmm... Doesn't look good..

Is it time to initiate the water-saving program?

Well.. I think we should try to reach **Frugal Faucet**.

I hope he'll see the signal.

KEEP OUT

FROM HIGH ATOP THEIR OFFICES, A BEAM OF LIGHT CUTS THE DARKNESS..

..A GIANT DRIP IS EMBLAZONED ON THE NIGHT SKY.

CAST YOUR FACE TO THE WINDOW

It's for you.

FRUGAL FAUCET, EVER-VIGILANT PROTECTOR OF THE CITY'S PRECIOUS WATER SUPPLY, PATROLS THE STREETS AS AN ORDINARY CITIZEN:

Aha!! Commercial sprinkler out of control! This calls for action!!

Is there another phone booth around here?

A couple down the street.

10-22-88

DRAT! Occupied! Maybe there's one around the corner!

FLASH-ER GORDON? Frank

911? I want to report a flasher..

And I don't even get paid for this..

HIGH ATOP A NORTH BEACH APARTMENT BUILDING:

HA HA!! I TOLD YOU SO!!

3-10-89

YOU LAUGHED AT ME... "FRUGAL FAUCET!! READ THE PAPERS LATELY?? MANDATORY WATER RATIONING!! ∴ NO NEW HOOK-UPS IN MARIN!!

Sixty per cent cutbacks on water for farmers!! You're not laughing **now**, are you??

© Phil (ABLE TO LEAP FROM TALL BUILDINGS)

I guess this is what happens when a superhero loses it..

NYAA!! NYAA!! NYAA!!

JUMP! JUMP!

Now that we have an official drought on our hands, I can wear my **Frugal Faucet** suit with pride!!

3-9-89

Aha! There's trouble! That's not smoke.. ..that's **steam**! Where there's steam, there's **water**!!

Thanks to my x-ray vision, I can see right through this glass shower door. This woman's using too much water!

AEII!! POW

© Phil (STEAM GETS IN YOUR EYE) FRANK

Remember.. Take shorter showers and be careful how you use that x-ray vision!

FRUGAL FAUCET, WATER SAVER, WORKS THE HOLIDAY CROWDS.

Help Conserve Water. Free brochures.

12-2-88

MEANWHILE AROUND THE CORNER A DIFFERENT WATER GROUP GIVES OUT **FLOW RESTRICTORS** TO PUT ON WATER FAUCETS AND CUT DOWN USAGE..

FREE FLOW RESTRICTORS!

Hi. You're **Frugal Faucet** aren't you!

Why, yes. I am.

© Phil (THE BIRTH OF A NOTION) FRANK

You should be giving out Flow restrictors too!

Hey! It's tough enough getting people to save water without getting into the birth control issue too!!

FRUGAL FAUCET DONS HIS UNIFORM TO RESPOND TO A WATER EMERGENCY:

I've got to get to that leaking reservoir or...

DING! DONG!

Drat! Who could that be?

What do you want at this hour of...

TRICK OR TR..

He gave me a Snickers bar.

(PHIL (BUT LIQUOR'S QUICKER.) Frank)

Hey!! Look who's here! It's Frugal Faucet.. Come in to get out of the rain, Frugal?

Haw!! Haw! Haw!!

I'd like a drink if you don't mind!

Gee.. I hope you don't want a scotch and WATER. You know we're in a big drought!

So.. have you heard the latest joke going around?

Can't say that I have..

(PHIL (A SIT DOWN COMEDIAN.) Frank)

Seems there was this traveling water salesman from Northern California who goes to this San Joaquin farmer's house..

This, too, shall pass..

FRUGAL FAUCET, SUPERHERO, BROODS IN HIS METROPOLITAN HIDEAWAY:

Nobody listens to me..

You've got a classic PR problem, Farley. Water conservation isn't a sexy issue..

You need to tie it in with something newsworthy... like dieting! Let's see... ..if a person doesn't drink the usual two quarts of water a day..

That's 3.5 pounds of water a day. Hey! You'd save water and lose 105 pounds in one month..

(PHIL (NO PAIN, NO GAIN.) Frank)

And you'd be dead!

True.. but you'd look great!!

Panel 1: THE NEWS IS NOT GOOD AT THE WATER DEPARTMENT:

The snow pack is 38% of normal..

Santa Clara's reservoir is only 10% of capacity.

Panel 2: We'd better take the lead and initiate a water conservation program now!

Us?.. Now?

Panel 3: If not now.. when? If not us.. who?

Yes, sir!

1-31-90

© Phil One Small Step For Man...Frank

Panel 4: The usual bourbon and water, gents?

Hold the water!

Panel 5: AT THE WATER DEPARTMENT:

I sure hope **Frugal Faucet** sees our signal!

CHIEF!! IT'S HIM!

2-2-90

Panel 6: FRUGAL! Thank heavens you saw the big drip! We have another water crisis pending! We need you to educate the public!!

Panel 7: So you need me to put on my silly outfit and convince people to conserve water?

Yes! Yes!

© Phil The Loan Arranger? Frank

Panel 8: You want new tights? ...travel expenses? ... a company car? and you want your plunger gold plated?.. YES! YES! We're writing this down!!

Panel 9: THE FORMER HERO OF THE LAST DROUGHT, PRESENTLY RETIRED, TRIES OUT HIS FRESHLY DRY-CLEANED UNIFORM.

Phew! I don't recall this fitting so tightly around the middle..

1-5-90

Panel 10: Maybe instead of water conservation you should've represented waist management!

Very funny, Bruce.. Now for the hat!

Panel 11: TA-DA!! **FRUGAL FAUCET,** FIGHTER OF WATER WASTE...at your service!

I'll be right back!

© Phil (Aviary Embarrassing Scene) Frank

Panel 12: Okay.. It's a dollar a peek and no laughing out loud!

Where are you going at this hour?

Out! There's a report of a suspicious person seen near the reservoir..

Take me with you, Frugal Faucet! Let me be your assistant!

I don't **need** an assistant!

2-12-90

Batman's assistant was Robin. Yours could be **Raven**! Please! Please!

No!

PLEASE, FRUGAL, PLEASE.. PLEASE.

Do other superheroes go through this?

©Phil (BIRD of PRAY) Frank

Take me with you,.. please!!

FRUGAL FAUCET works **alone**!

But, Frugal.. you **need** an assistant! I could be there to help if you got into trouble.

What kind of trouble could **I** possibly get in to?

2-13-90

Well, for one thing you can't fly.

Hmm.. He's got a point there..

©Phil (TALON SCOUT) Frank

Okay.. We're headed for the Crystal Springs Reservoir..

Me and my big beak..

THE CAPED CRUSADER, **FRUGAL FAUCET**, AND HIS OVERWORKED ASSISTANT FINALLY ARRIVE AT THE **CRYSTAL SPRINGS** RESERVOIR:

Take us down, Bruce.

2-15-90

A suspicious person has been around here... ..lurking near the City's water supply..

LOOK! a truck!

HOLY BINARY COMPOUNDS!! It's a truck delivering fluoride to add to the water supply!

FLUORIDE

©Phil (THE BEAST IS YET TO COME) Frank

Look, Bruce.. ..a figure is emerging from the shadows..

Why.. it's **another** caped crusader!

DRATS!! I'VE BEEN SCOOPED!

What superhero has scooped Frugal? Wendy Nelder is a City Supervisor whose pet crusade is getting fluoride out of our water!

THE TANKER TRUCK LOADED WITH FLUORIDE FOR THE CITY'S WATER SUPPLY SCREECHES TO A HALT.

SILHOUETTED IN THE HEAD-LIGHT GLARE STANDS THE CRUSADING OPPONENT OF FILTHY STREETS, MSG AND FLUORIDE IN THE CITY'S WATER.

2·16·90

WENDY WO'MAN!! WHO, DISGUISED AS A MILD-MANNERED MEMBER OF THE BOARD OF SUPERVISORS FIGHTS A...

AHEM!

BUT PERHAPS A BATTLE OF THE TITANS IS IN THE OFFING:

Hi! I'm Frugal Faucet.. superhero. I believe I was here first.

© Phil (OBEY A NELDER) Frank

EARTH DAY

FOG CITY REPERTORY COMPANY

The media is big on the "Earth Day" celebration as everyone gets conservation oriented.. for one day... then back to the old wasteful routine. The **Fog City Repertory Company** puts on a skit a la San Francisco Mime Troupe.

THE **FOG CITY REPERTORY COMPANY** IS DEEP IN REHEARSALS FOR THEIR EARTH DAY PERFORMANCE:

Okay.. quiet please! This is the beginning of Act II ..

DIRECTOR

4·10·90

"After millions of years of a peaceful planet, man evolves.. The Industrial Revolution arrives, and with it come toxins and pollution."

Enter Hilda as Mother Nature.

GRRRRRR! I'M MAD AS HELL AND I'M NOT GOING TO TAKE IT ANYMORE!

© Phil (A REAL MOTHER..) Frank

Um.. a bit of a heavy interpretation of the character, Hilda.. Try it again, with the primrose headband this time.

ECTOR

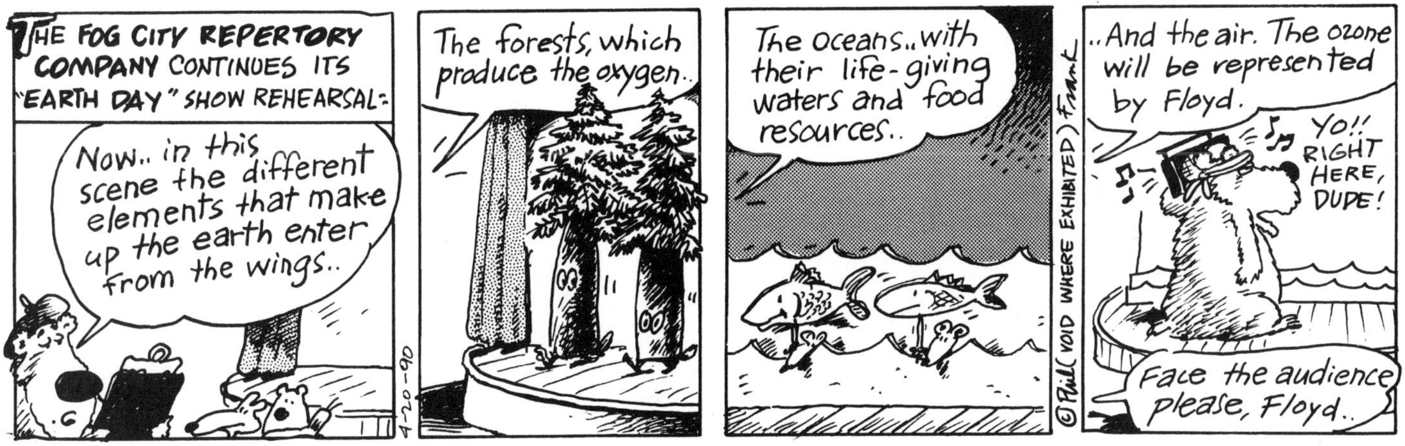
THE FOG CITY REPERTORY COMPANY CONTINUES ITS "EARTH DAY" SHOW REHEARSAL:
Now.. in this scene the different elements that make up the earth enter from the wings..
4-20-90
The forests, which produce the oxygen..
The oceans.. with their life-giving waters and food resources..
© Phil Frank (VOID WHERE EXHIBITED)
..And the air. The ozone will be represented by Floyd.
YO!! RIGHT HERE, DUDE!
Face the audience please, Floyd..

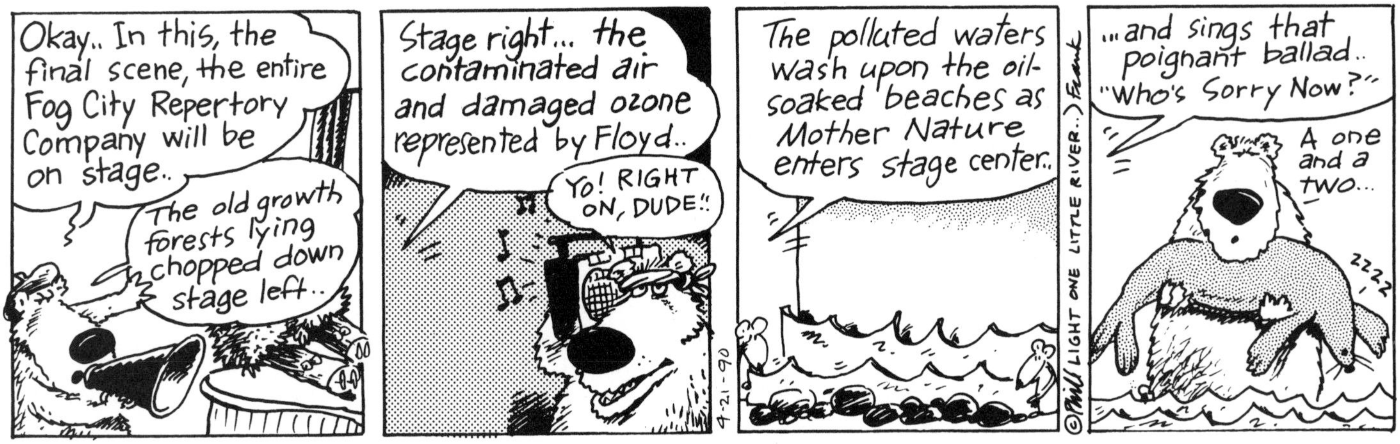
Okay.. In this, the final scene, the entire Fog City Repertory Company will be on stage..
The old growth forests lying chopped down stage left..
Stage right... the contaminated air and damaged ozone represented by Floyd..
YO! RIGHT ON, DUDE!
4-21-90
The polluted waters wash upon the oil-soaked beaches as Mother Nature enters stage center..
© Phil Frank (LIGHT ONE LITTLE RIVER..)
...and sings that poignant ballad.. "Who's Sorry Now?"
A one and a two...

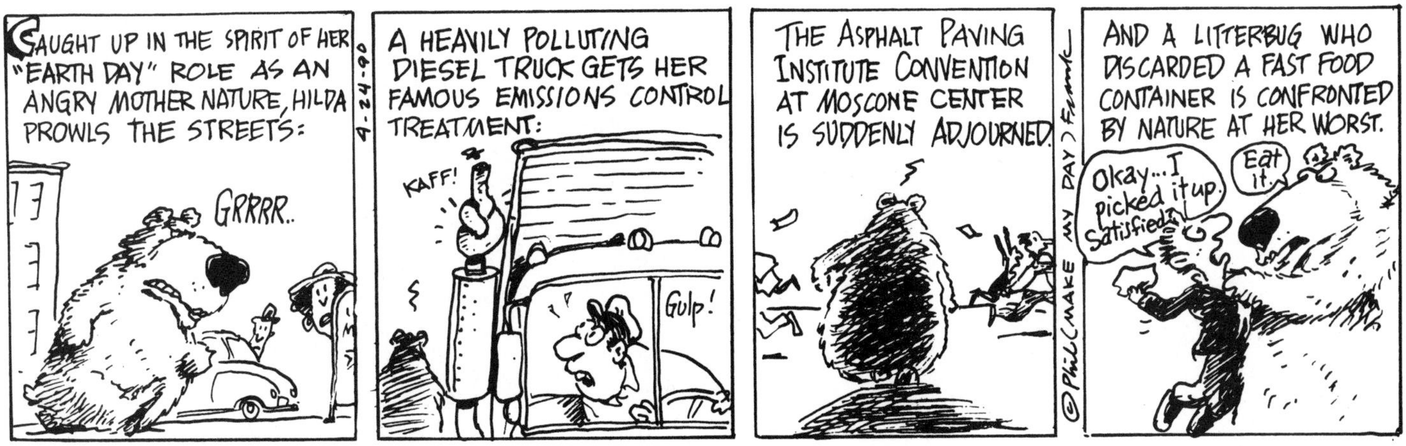
CAUGHT UP IN THE SPIRIT OF HER "EARTH DAY" ROLE AS AN ANGRY MOTHER NATURE, HILDA PROWLS THE STREETS:
GRRRR..
4-24-90
A HEAVILY POLLUTING DIESEL TRUCK GETS HER FAMOUS EMISSIONS CONTROL TREATMENT:
KAFF!
Gulp!
THE ASPHALT PAVING INSTITUTE CONVENTION AT MOSCONE CENTER IS SUDDENLY ADJOURNED.
© Phil Frank (MAKE MY DAY)
AND A LITTERBUG WHO DISCARDED A FAST FOOD CONTAINER IS CONFRONTED BY NATURE AT HER WORST.
Okay... I picked it up. Satisfied?
Eat it.

It IS THE MORNING AFTER **EARTH DAY** AND THE FINAL SPEAKER, SENATOR LIPSERVICE, WRAPS UP HIS COMMENTS:

Eternal vigilance will be our cry!!

Together we will free the ozone, mop up acid rain and preserve the spotted wood mouse..

We'll freeze the nuclears, ban all fluorocarbons, hydrocarbons and just plain carbons!

Rest assured that I shall be working day and night to save my..

..job!

GIVE CITY HALL THE BIRD!

Everyone else was running for office so why not a right-winged avian candidate? The response to Bruce D. Raven's candidacy was interesting. Contributions came in. Offers of graft and corruption poured in. Someone was stapling posters all over town... In the end I think he was glad he lost.

I've just been to City Hall to see who's presently in the race for mayor, Bruce...

Oh?

It seems that a certain unidentified black bird had just been in..

It's true. I've taken out the papers!

I lined my cage with them

Where you get the idea that **you** might ever be a candidate for mayor is beyond me, Bruce!

Oh?

3-11

It may not be as sewn up as you suppose. There's a lot of talk about a new candidate emerging..

© Phil THE GOSPEL ACCORDING TO BRUCE Frank

What.. a dark horse?

Or bird, as the case may be.

3-12

Now.. I'm not saying I **will** run for mayor. Taking out these papers is not an intention to join the race.

But, Bruce.. You have **no** constituency out there!

What?.. Are there no animal lovers..

..right-wingers or flighty voters in this city?

© Phil (ON A WING AND A PRAYER) Frank

Hmm..

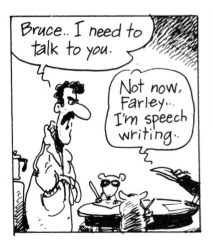

Bruce.. I need to talk to you.

Not now, Farley.. I'm speech writing..

Bruce... I want you to cut out this nonsense about running for mayor.

Why?

10-3-87

Because you're not human. You're a raven.. a cunning, opportunistic, unpredictable bird with... with...

With what?

© Phil (ane asylum) Frank

..with all the necessary qualifications, come to think of it.

Yet another vote!

ON THE SET OF AN UP-AND-COMING MAYORAL CANDIDATE'S NEW TV SPOT:

So... what do I have to do, Walter?

MAKE UP

8-20

It's easy, Bruce.. you walk down Market Street and tell people how tough you are.. ..How you ruffle feathers but get things done.

Then what?

That's it.

You mean I just talk? I don't **do** anything?

Not if you want a long career in politics..

©Phil (A CHICKEN ON EVERY POT) Frank

Walter.. I'm not sure I can do this tough-guy routine...

Bruce D. Raven
One Tough Bird
TAKE! 5

8-21

I mean... I'm a gentle bird..

Bruce, baby! That's politics! You gotta make yourself up to appeal to voters.

I don't mind the part where I ruffle the feathers or step on the paws to get things done... ..but..

But what?

©Phil (BOAS CONSTRICTOR) Frank

If I kick this asp one more time, he's done for!

Props! Another snake!

WHILE CASUALLY PERUSING HIS CAGE LINER, BRUCE NOTICES AN INTERESTING HEADLINE:

"S.F. Conservatives Seek Candidate!" I gotta call these guys.."

7-7

Hey.. I could be your candidate!! I've already been endorsed by the "John Perch Society"..

"The National Cannon Owners".. ..The "Mothers for a Military-Industrial Complex.. umm.. "Ban the Poor" and the "Peace Later Society."

And on the _far_ right, I have...

CLICK!

©Phil ('BYE 'BYE, BLACKBIRD) Frank

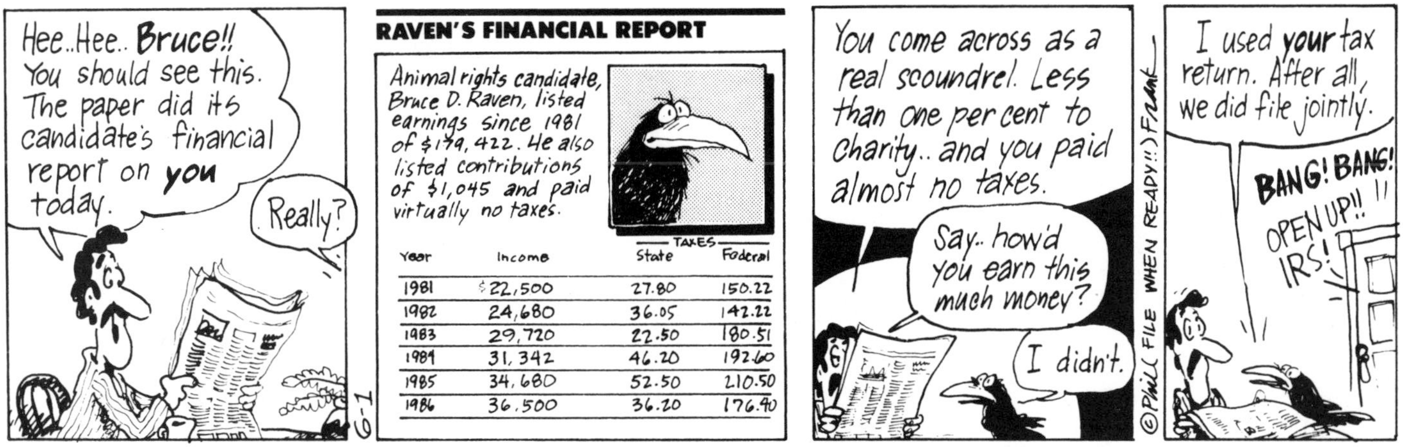
Hee..Hee.. Bruce!! You should see this. The paper did its candidate's financial report on you today.
Really?
RAVEN'S FINANCIAL REPORT
Animal rights candidate, Bruce D. Raven, listed earnings since 1981 of $179,422. He also listed contributions of $1,045 and paid virtually no taxes.
TAXES
Year Income State Federal
1981 $22,500 27.80 150.22
1982 24,680 36.05 142.22
1983 29,720 22.50 180.51
1984 31,342 46.20 192.60
1985 34,680 52.50 210.50
1986 36,500 36.20 176.40
You come across as a real scoundrel. Less than one per cent to charity.. and you paid almost no taxes.
Say.. how'd you earn this much money?
I didn't.
I used your tax return. After all, we did file jointly.
BANG! BANG!
OPEN UP!! IRS!
6-1
©Phil (FILE WHEN READY!!) Frank

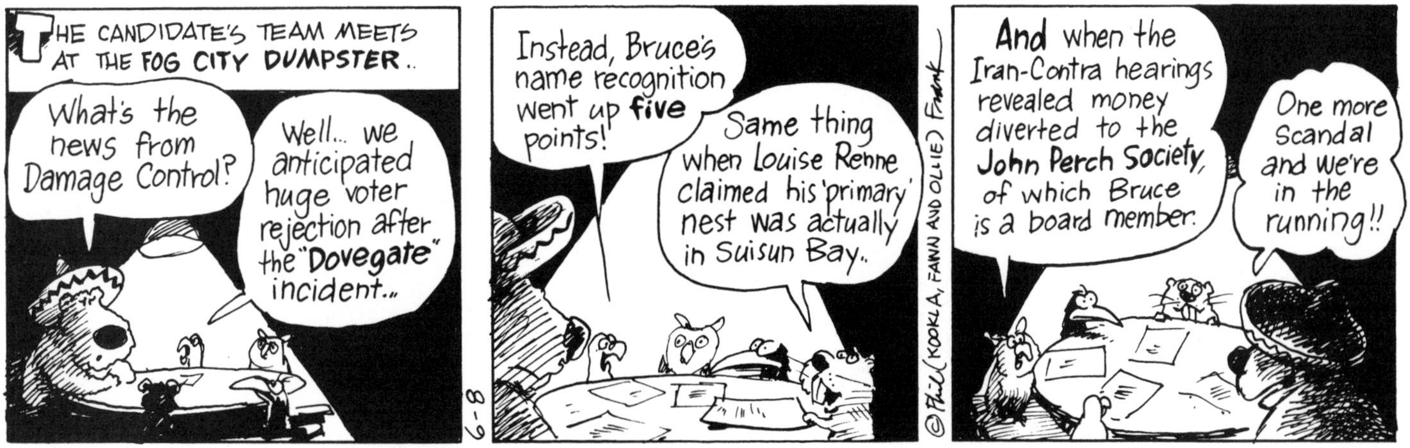
THE CANDIDATE'S TEAM MEETS AT THE FOG CITY DUMPSTER..
What's the news from Damage Control?
Well... we anticipated huge voter rejection after the "Dovegate" incident..
Instead, Bruce's name recognition went up five points!
Same thing when Louise Renne claimed his 'primary' nest was actually in Suisun Bay..
And when the Iran-Contra hearings revealed money diverted to the John Perch Society, of which Bruce is a board member.
One more Scandal and we're in the running!!
6-8
©Phil (KOOKLA, FAWN AND OLLIE) Frank

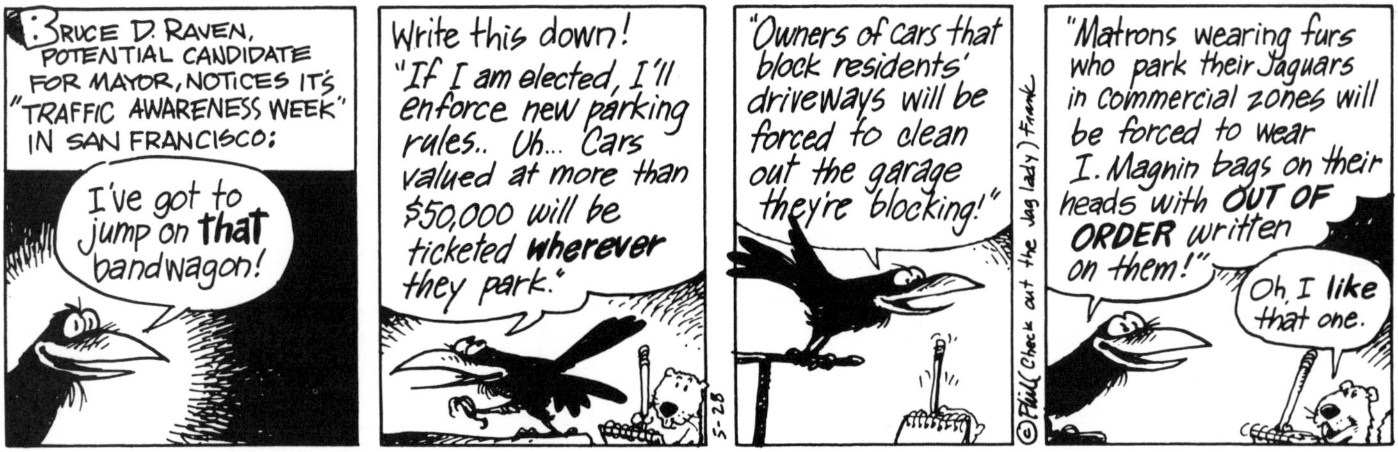
BRUCE D. RAVEN, POTENTIAL CANDIDATE FOR MAYOR, NOTICES IT'S "TRAFFIC AWARENESS WEEK" IN SAN FRANCISCO:
I've got to jump on that bandwagon!
Write this down! "If I am elected, I'll enforce new parking rules.. Uh... Cars valued at more than $50,000 will be ticketed wherever they park."
"Owners of cars that block residents' driveways will be forced to clean out the garage they're blocking!"
"Matrons wearing furs who park their Jaguars in commercial zones will be forced to wear I. Magnin bags on their heads with OUT OF ORDER written on them!"
Oh, I like that one.
5-28
©Phil (Check out the Jag lady) Frank

AT THE $100-A-PERCH DINNER FOR THE MAYORAL CANDIDATE AT THE FAIRMONT'S TALON ROOM:

So nice to see you all here...

What a sight...robins from the Richmond, sparrows from the Sunset...parrots, gulls, canaries, egrets...

GIVE CITY HALL The BIRD

7-20

And last but not least in the pecking order...

© Phil (CHEEP SHOT) Frank

...our friends from the financial district.

CITY HALL!

Mr. Raven... Where do you stand on the downtown stadium?

The big issue here once again is parking.

1-8

Rather than treating the cars as a handicap we will make them an asset with **my** proposal.

GIVE CIT HALL TH BIRD!

San Francisco will have the first major league drive-in baseball park!

HONK FOR A HIT!

©Phil (HOOOOONK BABY!) Frank

Two Polish dogs and a frozen malt?

Mr. Raven.. we are familiar with your political stands on property rights, traffic, parking and dirty streets...but what about other voter concerns?

GIVE CITY THI BIR

11/6

You have failed to address long-term issues such as nuclear power, acid rain, air quality and recycling...

What we want to know is what you intend to do for future generations?

©Phil (THE PAST IS YET TO COME?) Frank

Hey! What have the future generations ever done for **me**?

Gee.. I never realized running for mayor could be so expensive. Look at these bills..

GIVE CITY HALL THE BIRD

Here's another one, Bruce.

What's this for?

Oh.. just some office supplies.

Paper clips.. $2.50
Tape $1.39
Staples ..$602.48

Six hundred dollars worth of staples?

So.. one of a bear's staples happens to be salmon.

© Phil (A REAL CHINOOK) Frank

AT THE CAMPAIGN HEADQUARTERS OF **BRUCE D. RAVEN** ON BEAVER STREET... THE CANDIDATE THROWS A FIT..

MY PROPOSAL"

BRUCE D. RAVEN FOR **MAYOR**

The downtown stadium was **my** proposal! I was pushing it in **my** campaign. **Now** the supes put it on the ballot. I've been **robbed**!!

Someone in here is... is leaking information to my rivals!

GIVE CIT HALL THE

© Phil (DON'T ROCK THE VOTE!) Frank

And... Who stole the strawberries?!

"Captain Queeg Syndrome" setting in a bit early this election...

AT A CANDIDATE BREAKFAST:

Mr. Raven.. How would you, as Mayor, deal with the issue of the homeporting of the USS Missouri?

Drat! I've been dreading that question..

On the one wing...
..it'll mean lots of much-needed jobs on the waterfront..
..plenty of tax dollars..

But.. on the other wing..
..it means a nuclear presence on the bay, massive dredging and making the city a target for attack.

My course is clear!

Um.. I'd tend towards a definite maybe on that.. ..perhaps.

Who ordered the waffle?

© Phil (A RAVENOUS APPETITE) Frank

OFFHAND MANOR

Could you stop preening your royal plumage for a minute?

Would you like an audience?

Cute. Listen, millet-breath, you'd better start paying attention to your chores around here!

Chores?? Farley.. mayoral candidates don't **do** chores..

8-22

At least not voluntarily..

© Phil (Pardon my dust) Frank

THE MAYORAL CANDIDATE MEETS THE PRESS:

The most pressing concern amongst citizens is traffic and its related problems..

7-28

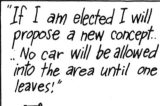

"If I am elected I will propose a new concept.. ..No car will be allowed into the area until one leaves!"

SORRY FULL

"Cars valued at more than $50,000 will be ticketed **wherever** they're parked!"

© Phil (Born Toulouse) Frank

"**And** I will establish special parking zones for unemployed artists."

MAUVE ZONE 90 DAY PARKING

Hey! Where are you going with my tie?

To the Festa Italiana at Fisherman's Wharf. I'm a guest speaker.

You? You're not Italian!

True... but I **am** a politician.

© Phil (Well, Scuuuuusa me!) Frank

10-2-97

Buon giorno! Que pasa, mes amigos Italiano? I just flew in from Ravenna... ...and boy, are my arms tired. But seriously..

? ? GROOOAN

WE WANT SERGIO FRANCHI!

Do you have any stand on unapproved in-law units, Mr. Raven?

You bet I do!

Certain mayoral candidates want to make the in-law units all over the City illegal.

You're opposed to that?

Yes! I raise my right wing in protest!! I'm for property rights! People have a right to do whatever they want with their property!

"WHEN IN-LAWS ARE OUTLAWED ONLY OUTLAWS WILL HAVE IN-LAWS!!"

Is that how it goes?

I think you got it.

10-13-87

©Phil (Relatively speaking, that is) Frank

A few weeks ago I had doubts about this race but now I think we can win it..

What dedication!

Look at these statistics! Each of the other challengers lack something..

What a team!

Looks like my campaign is in good hands. I'm off to the "Friends of the Feathered" dinner..

I say the Giants sweep the Series in four games.

You're on!

9-10

©Phil (The Astro-Not) Frank

Eventually the election happens and with it the inevitable.

Bruce!! It's Farley.. are you there?.

I'm here.

I'm contacting every candidate in the recent election to see which of the two run-off contenders they will support..

..So, to whom will you throw the full weight of your... ..um.. fifty-two write-in votes?

Sometimes I just hate him..

Well?

12-1-87

©Phil (Place your pecking order here) Frank

"O pun the window!!"

Bad puns are not for daily consumption but on an occasional basis, when the barometer reading is good and the tide is out, I have chosen to lay some real groaners on my audience. A number of them have come in from readers so I cannot claim, nor be blamed for, the authorship of all of them.

WARNING

READERS ARE CAUTIONED THAT THE FOLLOWING COMIC STRIP CONTAINS AN ATROCIOUS PUN. VIEWER DISCRETION IS RECOMMENDED.

THE REPORTER REVIEWS A NEW COMMERCIAL ESTABLISHMENT FOR THE BUSINESS SECTION:

SURREAL HANDTRUCKS

ART FOR THE WORKPLACE

If I may be of any help..

?

Uh... what's *this* one?

Ah... *that* one..

That's our Salvador Dolly.

©Phil (HEY! YOU WERE WARNED...) Frank

THE BIRDS' SOCIAL SEASON IS UNDERWAY AMIDST THE FERMENTING PYRACANTHA BERRY BUSHES OF TELEGRAPH HILL:

OOO...SOLE MEOW!!

A DARK SHADOW SWEEPS LOW AND SUDDENLY ALL'S SILENT.

Who's in charge here?

Uh.. I guess I am..

You're in a heap of trouble, boy. I'm takin' you in on a 482!

A 482?

Yeah. Contributing to the delinquency of a mynah.

GULP!

I'm outta here.

©Phil (WILL THE PUN NEVER STOP?) Frank

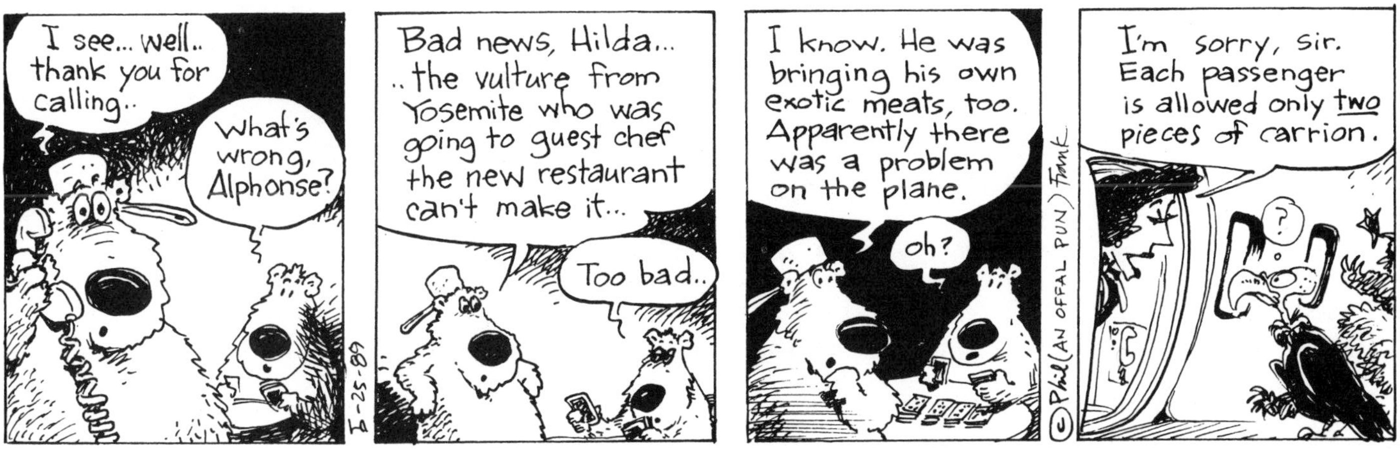
I see... well.. thank you for calling..
What's wrong, Alphonse?
1-25-89
Bad news, Hilda... ..the vulture from Yosemite who was going to guest chef the new restaurant can't make it...
Too bad..
I know. He was bringing his own exotic meats, too. Apparently there was a problem on the plane.
oh?
© Phil (AN OFFAL PUN) Frank
I'm sorry, sir. Each passenger is allowed only two pieces of carrion.
?

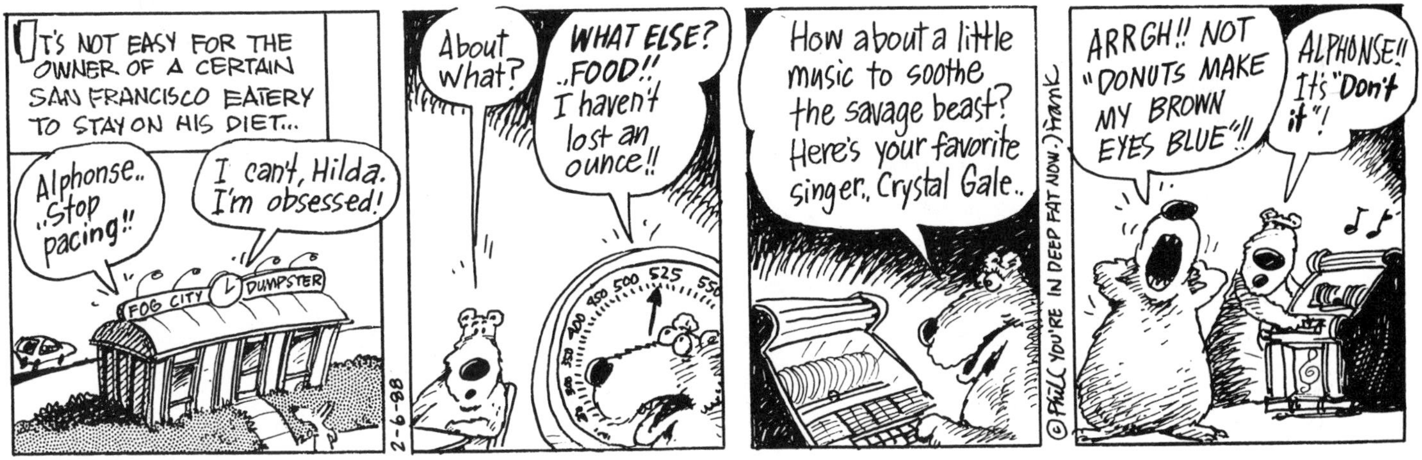
IT'S NOT EASY FOR THE OWNER OF A CERTAIN SAN FRANCISCO EATERY TO STAY ON HIS DIET...
Alphonse.. ..Stop pacing!!
I can't, Hilda. I'm obsessed!
FOG CITY DUMPSTER
2-6-88
About what?
WHAT ELSE? ..FOOD!! I haven't lost an ounce!!
500 525 550
How about a little music to soothe the savage beast? Here's your favorite singer.. Crystal Gale..
© Phil (YOU'RE IN DEEP FAT NOW.) Frank
ARRGH!! NOT "DONUTS MAKE MY BROWN EYES BLUE"!!
ALPHONSE!! It's "Don't it"!

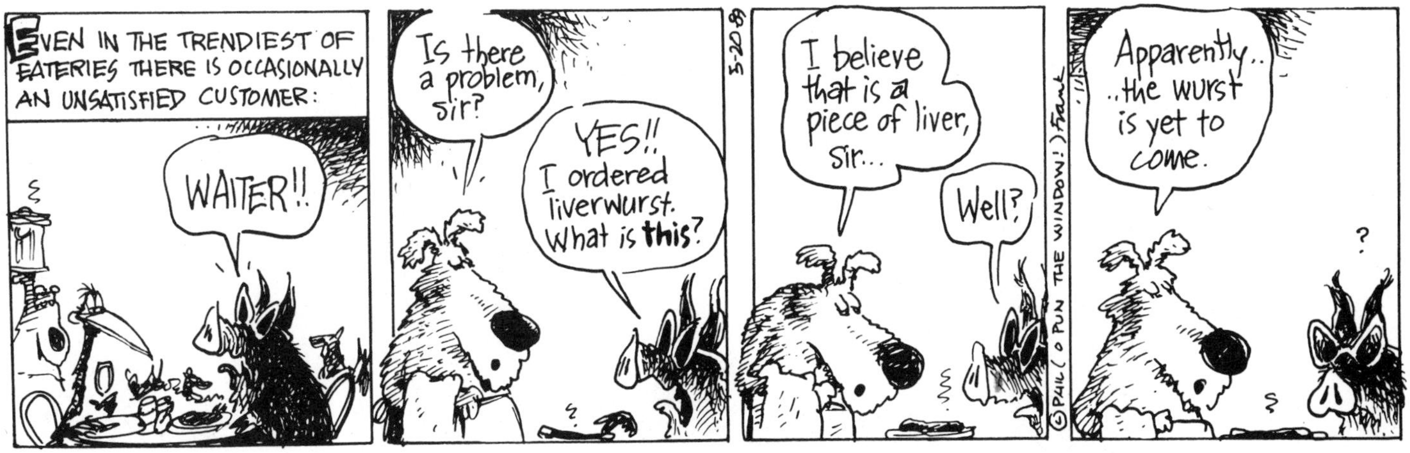
EVEN IN THE TRENDIEST OF EATERIES THERE IS OCCASIONALLY AN UNSATISFIED CUSTOMER:
WAITER!!
3-20-88
Is there a problem, sir?
YES!! I ordered liverwurst. What is this?
I believe that is a piece of liver, sir...
Well?
© Phil (O PUN THE WINDOW!) Frank
Apparently.. ..the wurst is yet to come.
?

San Francisco Week

It was to be "San Francisco Week" in Hong Kong. We were shipping over a cable car, a softball team, emissaries and dignitaries. How could I resist? I couldn't!

Farley watches as three **MUNI** buses are loaded aboard an Asia-bound freighter..

The transit system's precision bus squadron is on its way to "**SAN FRANCISCO WEEK**" in Hong Kong.

Muni's "**ORANGE ANGELS**" will be performing on February 11th..

The famous **CALTRANS** "**ROUGH ROADERS**" traffic diversion unit will appear on the 12th..

PLANNERS FOR THE UPCOMING "SAN FRANCISCO WEEK" IN HONG KONG DISCUSS LAST-MINUTE DETAILS..

We need to think of an appropriate gift for our hosts...

2-3-88

What do we have in common besides culture and geography?

Well... ..houseboats.

In fact, the Sausalito City Council is proposing a novel exchange program...

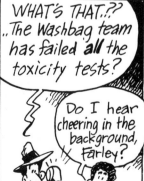

You won't get rid of us **this** easily, capitalist lackeys!!

© PHIL (THERE GOES THE NEIGHBORHOOD) FRANK

IT'S "SAN FRANCISCO WEEK" IN HONG KONG AND FORMER MAYOR DIANNE FEINSTEIN INITIATES OPENING CEREMONIES:

Join me in welcoming Muni's crack bus squadron.. ...the Orange Angels!!

CLAP!! CLAP!! CLAP!! CLAP!!

2-8-88

Once again... let's welcome those precision drivers... ..."**The Orange Angels**"!!

CLAP!! CLAP!! CLAP!! CLAP!!

© PHIL (CALL BELL-TOOL) FRANK

Once!!.. just **once** they could be on time!...

OUR REPORTER HAS A DIRECT PHONE HOOK-UP TO THE "SAN FRANCISCO WEEK" FESTIVITIES IN HONG KONG..

The girls' chorus is just finishing the National Anthem?

2-9-88

Right... now the softball teams come onto the field..

According to international sports laws, the Washington Square and Hong Kong teams are presenting their specimen bottles to the officials..

© PHIL (JUST SAY... MAYBE) FRANK

WHAT'S THAT..??
..The Washbag team has failed **all** the toxicity tests?

Do I hear cheering in the background, Farley?

You are Cordially Invited
to the Gala Opening
of the 1986-87
San Francisco Political Opera
at
The Southern Pacific
Memorial Opera House
and Stadium
SEVENTH & TOWNSEND
Black Tie (Spikes Optional)

A downtown site has been located for a Giants stadium, something Dianne Feinstein wholeheartedly supports but which the owner of the Giants, Bob Lurie, is cool about. The site is a Southern Pacific train yard. It is a cold and windy place...but it **is** downtown. The intrigue surrounding this issue is like a comic opera so I cast the characters in their respective roles, little suspecting that I too will become enmeshed in the unfolding drama.

A COLD WINDBLOWN FIELD...
..ENTER THE CONTESSA DIANA DE FEINSTEIN AND HER RETINUE..

Contessa.. We have arrived.♪

WE HAVE ARRIVED.. WE HAVE ARRIVED.

Oh Sacred Place...♪ Oh Hallowed Ground... I honor thee with my feet...

WE ARE HERE!! WE ARE HERE!!

Oh Sacred Place Where one day a stadium♪ will stand... Bid the torches light. Bid the candles stick.!!

WE ARE FREEZING! WE ARE FREEZING!

©Phil (MANY ARE COLD BUT BEWARE FROZEN) Frank

In this, Act II of the political Opera, the Contessa Diana De Feinstein awaits the arrival of Prince Roberto De Luria...

She stands on the parcel she intends to grant to the prince. Here the royal games will be conducted... The curtain rises...

♪ Oh Roberto...

Roberto! Roberto!

5-27

Hark!! Afar ♪ I see a light!!

She sees a light! She sees a light!!

©Phil (LET'S MAKE TRACKS) Frank

♪ It's a train!! ♪

RUN FOR IT! RUN FOR IT!

ACT III Prince Roberto De Luria has at last arrived and is shown the grounds for the royal games by the Contessa De Feinstein...

This is the land whereof thou speaks, milady?

It is but a windswept desolate piece of terra infirma crossed by tracks of the iron horse. I desire fairer land than this.

5-28

WHAT?

♪ IT'S HITTING THE FAN! IT'S HITTING THE FAN!! ♪

©Phil (Hard Hat Aria) Frank

WHAT??

I read the front page headlines with alarm!! Bob Lurie had just sent a letter to Mayor Feinstein indicating he'd support a stadium at this windswept site. Meanwhile in the cartoon I have him scoffing at the location. In the next day's strip the Mayor, angry, sends the Prince off to his dungeon — the really cold Candlestick Stadium which his team presently occupies. I hopped in my car and sped to the paper to change the next day's strip. I substituted a new panel to replace the original last panel.

Ⓑ

Sebben, crudele, mi fai languir, sempre fedele, ti voglio amar....

Tho' not deserving thy cruel scorn, Ever unswerving, thee only I love..

Con la lunghezza del mio servir la tua fierezza saprò stancar.

When to thee kneeling All I have borne, Thy pride unfeeling I then shall move.

Ⓐ The original panel:

To Candlestick with thee!!

To Candlestick with thee!!

©Phil (Bob be nimble...Bob be quick) Frank

Substitute panel:

Of course, 'tis not the final out...

Let's make a deal.

Ⓒ

This strip I completely rewrote to match the unfolding drama.

ACT V..The Contessa De Feinstein, her offer of land to Prince Roberto De Luria coolly met lashes out:

IT'S NO FUN BEING AN ACTOR.. ESPECIALLY WITH THIS WIND-CHILL FACTOR!

MARK ME WELL. ACCEPT THIS LAND OR BE BANISHED TO CANDLESTICK!

Aha! My plan doth work. Mine princely foot-dragging will concessions bring from Queen and voters both.

He's sprung the trap, He's closed the lid, you really got to like this kid!

©Frank (LEAVE IT TO DIVA)

The final strip was originally to read like this:

THE PLAYERS HAVE ALL EXITED THE 7th AND TOWNSEND STAGE, LEAVING ONLY THE BROODING CONTESSA DIANA AND HER JESTER..

What fickle men these be!

Thou speaks the truth, fair mistress..

Thou hast offered to construct a giant stadium for Prince Roberto De Luria and been rejected. There is but one thing to do..

©Frank (AUTHOR! AUTHOR!)

And what be that, Jester?

Let's go to Perry's for a beer.

CLAP!!
CLAP!!
CLAP!!
CLAP!!
BRAVO!!
CLAP!!

I was able to save the majority of the strip by changing the copy which the Contessa's spiritual guide whispers in her ear.

The Prince doth toy with thy affections... We cannot bend the future to our will.. However there is one thing we **can** do...

I kept the last panel as it was and, exhausted took Baba's advice:

I'm going to Perry's for a beer!

Dianne's tenure as mayor is coming to an end. She was swept into office by the death of Mayor George Moscone, grew into the position and was now looking beyond San Francisco for a political future.

INSIDE THE OFFICE OF THE MAYOR OF SAN FRANCISCO:

Madam mayor...As your adviser I feel that allowing an outsider into your..

What.. a bird?

You worry too much! Besides, I like the way he sits, brooding, on that bust of Pallas..

Now begone!! I wish to be alone to think about political fortunes!

©PHIL PALLAS OF FINE ART/Frank

Mayor.. Mayor.. on the wall.. who's the fairest candidate of all?

Can you believe this?

Journalists had dubbed Dianne the "Ice Queen", suggesting she'd rather hold the political position of Queen than mayor or governor. As she was considering her political future, she had a dream:

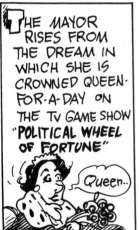

THE MAYOR RISES FROM THE DREAM IN WHICH SHE IS CROWNED QUEEN-FOR-A-DAY ON THE TV GAME SHOW "POLITICAL WHEEL OF FORTUNE"

Queen..

Ohh.. Mirror.. I'm Queen!

Only for a day, my lady..

You know... I **really** like the feel of ermine....

©PHIL (WHEN IT REIGNS...IT POURS) Frank

Oh, mirror... Could I be Queen-for-a Day **every** day?

Uh... I'll have to get back to you on that..

And so the footlights fade on Dianne's term of office as mayor. A new head of government is about to be elected by San Franciscans.

Why feral pigs??...an often-asked question. I'd been reading numerous stories in the paper about the destructive habits and rude behavior of an estimated 1,000 pigs that were terrorizing Bay Area watersheds with their rooting and rutting. In none of the articles was there a photo to justify the calculated hordes. The paper suggested they were too elusive to photograph. I suggested they were so elusive because there were not 1,000 doing all this damage but rather four of them in a BMW.

SNORK!

This is going to be a lousy story about West Marin's feral pigs if this is all you can show me.. Some overturned earth

Well.. they're very elusive.

11-5

It's not like you can arrange an interview and photo session. They're very hard to spot. You'd need an airplane to do that.

An airplane?

Hmm..

?

SAFARI SO GOOD? Frank

Uh.. This is Porker Patrol. I'm now over pig country. Do you read me?

FARLEY PURSUES THE WEST MARIN FERAL PIG STORY..

Scoop calling Foxtrot. Do you read me?

ROGER! I READ YOU LOUD AND CLEAR!

11-6

You are looking for a pack of feral pigs.. They'll be rooting up the landscape.

Any signs of pigs? Over.

This is Foxtrot. I may have something!

AISLE 2-B or NOT 2-B...Frank

The Palace Market in Point Reyes has a special on bacon.

THE AERIAL RECONNAISSANCE UNIT DRIFTS LAZILY OVER THE WEST MARIN LANDSCAPE, SCANNING THE HORIZON FOR FERAL PIGS..

It's nice to get out to the country..

The pot searches are over so I won't get shot at..

WHOA! WHAT'S THAT?

THIS IS 'FOXTROT' CALLING FARLEY.. FOUR FERAL PIGS TEARING UP THE GROUND!

They're headed south towards Olema. Set up a roadblock. Over.

Uh.. Did you say roadblock? Over.

ROGER! THEY'RE DRIVING A WHITE BMW WITH VANITY PLATES. OVER.

©PHIL (BEWARE OF ROADHOGS) FRANK

THE SEARCH FOR THE ELUSIVE AND DESTRUCTIVE WEST MARIN FERAL PIGS CONTINUES.

Can I see your license, Sir..

Here you go, officer. Anything wrong?

©PHIL (AWASH AND AWARE) FRANK

We've had a lot of reports of feral pigs tearing up the landscape and we can't be too careful. Where are you folks headed?

Uh.. a.. Self-awareness seminar in Inverness.

THE HIGHWAY PATROL HAS STOPPED A BMW IN WEST MARIN..

Well.. everything is in order. You can go.

Thanks, officer. And good luck catching those feral pigs. They're a menace.

Drive safely. Uh.. where did you say you were going?

To uh.. a.. Self-actualization seminar. We'll learn greed, avarice and selfishness in one session.

Whew! That was a close one.

Lousy yuppies.

©PHIL (I WANT IT ALL NOW) FRANK

The pigs serve a secondary purpose of being my "bad boys" for those occasions where I require characters that are socially abhorrent, such as obnoxious diners, people who park in handicapped zones, rude drivers (FERAL EXPRESS), personal injury lawyers (DILLY, DALLY, DOLITTLE & STAHL), owners of a bankrupt S&L (FERAL SAVINGS & LOAN), drivers of tour buses (ROADHOGZ TOURS) and loud talkers at the opera (PORKY AND BESS). They have served me well.

Hey, baby! Let's get feral!

THE PIG PLAGUE

A DAILY REQUIREMENT FIVE PART SERIES...

SEE THE HAVOC WREAKED ON MARIN COUNTY BY THE RAPACIOUS FERAL PIGS!!

WELCOME TO MARIN COUNTY

SNURF!

2-23

WITNESS THE MIGRATION OF THESE PORCINE PLUNDERERS TO SAN FRANCISCO.

DANG! IT'S A $2 DAY!

SEETHE IN ANGER AS THESE RUDE ROADHOGS TAKE UP TWO LEGAL PARKING SPACES ON CLEMENT STREET.

BURP!

CRINGE IN TERROR AS THEY FLAUNT CIVIC AUTHORITY BY RINGING THE CITY ATTORNEY'S DOORBELL AND RUNNING AWAY!

© PHIL (HAM BONE, HAMBONE, WHERE YOU BEEN?) FRANK

WHO'S THERE?

THE PIG PLAGUE

WHERE DID THEY COME FROM?

CALIFORNIA OR BUST!

YEARS AGO WILD PIGS WERE BROUGHT TO CALIFORNIA FOR GAME HUNTING.

PUCKATA.. PUCKATA..

2-24

THEIR RANKS GREW AS ESCAPED DOMESTIC PIGS JOINED.

Who's the new guy?

BECAUSE THEY ARE RAPID BREEDERS, OFTEN PRODUCING TWO LITTERS A YEAR, THEIR NUMBERS HAVE INCREASED DRAMATICALLY..

Here are some pictures of my 832 grandchildren..

© PHIL (PORKLIPS NOW!) FRANK

THE PIG PLAGUE

WHY FERAL PIGS ARE SUCH A MENACE:

They're walking garbage cans!

2-25

They attack the earth like rototillers. They'll eat anything!..

SNURF!! SNURF!!

..Bulbs, earthworms, salamanders, acorns, mushrooms, rotting fruit..

PASS THE NUTS, PLEASE!

PIG OUT!

Their destructive habits are inbred and unchangeable.

As Ben Franklin said:.. "Show me your friends and I'll tell you what you are!"

SNORK!

© Phil THIS BUG'S FOR YOU! Frank

THE PIG PLAGUE

PART 4: HOW DO THEIR RANKS INCREASE?

SCREECH!

Hey, dude! We're going out to root for acorns and tear up the place. Want to come?

2-27

Oh, gee.. I don't think so.. It's real nice here. They feed us a lot and they said they're taking us on a field trip to a market soon..

Oh.. mahnn..

© Phil UN-PORCINE CIRCUMSTANCES/Frank

Be seein' you at Leon's Barbecue, SUCKER!!

?

THE PIG PLAGUE

2-26

EFFORTS TO CONTROL: Indiscriminate rooting by feral pigs has wreaked havoc on the environment in Marin County.

SNURF!

Hunting and trapping as a control has had minimal success.

Wait here. I'll get the wirecutters.

Now, in desperation, park rangers are trying to thwart migration by erecting 7 miles of fence.

© Phil C GIMME PIG) Frank

However, this tactic will only be effective on feral pigs that do not hold a valid California driver's license.

Gimme another root beer!

PIGS R US

THE PIG PLAGUE
MIGRATION HABITS

Coming up on the toll plaza. Fright wigs!!

2-28

Their movements are now being traced southward from Marin County.

Thank you!

This news story says 150 feral pigs have ended up at St. Anthony's for dinner.

For dinner?

GREAT! I'm starved.

Hang a right on Golden Gate.

©Phil (HAM ON WRY) Frank

THE INFAMOUS FERAL PIGS, BORED WITH RURAL LIFE, REAPPEAR IN SAN FRANCISCO FOR A NIGHT AT THE MOVIES:

"So.. where you wanna go?"

"I dunno... ..where **you** wanna go?"

"MARTY" starring Ernest Borghine!

2-26-88

"You boys lookin' for trouble?"

"Sure. Whaddaya got?"

"THE WILD ONES" starring Marlon Brando!

"Freda... I have to tell you.. ..I'm going back to my wife. We're through."

"You'll pay for this, Chauvinist Pig!"

Wasn't that "Feral Attraction" with what's-her-name?

©Phil (THE BORE WAR) Frank

WHITE BMW WITH VANITY PLATES SITS PARKED IN A HANDICAPPED ZONE IN FRONT OF ONE OF THE CITY'S TONIER RESTAURANTS..

,,THE FERAL PIGS ARE WALLOWING IN AN AFTER-THEATER DINNER AT **TRAINER VIC'S**..

YO, WAITER!! A MAGNUM OF YOUR FINEST FRENCH ROOT BEER!

MAKE THAT **TWO**, DUDE!

2-27-88

Those people are **SO** rude.

Typical nouveau riche!

Really? ..how can you tell?

Didn't you catch the gold nose rings?

SNORK! SNORK!

©Phil (THE ROOT OF ALL EVIL) Frank

THE FERAL PIGS, FRESH FROM THE WILDERNESS EXPERIENCE, HAVE INVADED THE CITY'S SOUTH OF MARKET AREA:

I hope we can get in this dump.

CLUB VERT-A-BR8

NO WORMS ALLOWED

3-12-88

YO! YOU THREE DUDES WITH THE NOSE RINGS.. ..YOU'RE IN!

ALL RIGHT!

Man.. they let anything in here..

I'm going to powder my snout. See you in the salad bar.

Gee.. it's been twenty minutes. Where is she?

SNORK!

© PHIL (TURNING OVER A NEW LEAF) FRANK

A WHITE BMW IS PARKED ILLEGALLY IN A HANDICAPPED ZONE IN FRONT OF HERBST THEATRE..

IT'S EASILY IDENTIFIED AS BELONGING TO THOSE ARBITERS OF BAD TASTE...THE WILD PIGS OF WEST MARIN..

CALIFORNIA
PIGS R US

HONK IF YOU'RE FERAL.

6-3-88

WHILE INSIDE:

FLAMENCO DANCERS?

SHHH! SHHH!

© PHIL (THE ROOTING SECTION) FRANK

I COULD'VE SWORN THE AD SAID "SWINE LAKE"

SHHHH!

THE FERAL PIGS SIT BESIDE THEIR BMW AND READ THE THEATER REVIEWS IN THE MORNING PAPER:

Listen to this..

"The Friday performance of Flamenco dancing at Herbst Hall was sublime, marred only by rowdies in the audience..

6-6-88

"..a noisy, bothersome group of feral pigs whose behavior was, as always, a paragon of bad taste."

Hey, we don't have bad taste..

© PHIL (LIVE AND LOIN.) FRANK

Yeah! We just taste bad!!

YUCK!! YUCK!!

SNORK! SNORK!

THEY'RE BIG..
THEY'RE BAD...
& THEY'RE BACK!

PORKLIPS NOW!

THE COMIC STRIP

SEE.. THE WILD PIGS RUN AMOK THROUGH A "SHARPER IMAGE" STORE...

Hey.. check out the computerized barbecues!

Man.. you're sick!

CRINGE.. IN TERROR OF **FERAL EXPRESS** DRIVERS LOOSE IN THE STREETS..

SCREEE

WATCH IN AWE AS THE COMMON ROAD HOG MEETS HIS MASTER!

BEEEEE!!

STOP

THE COOL FOG SNAKES ITS WAY OVER THE SUN-BAKED LANDSCAPE OF WEST MARIN..

.. THE FERAL PIGS WHO HAD PREVIOUSLY OVERRUN THESE VERDANT HILLS ARE NOWHERE TO BE SEEN..

.. BUT RESIDENT AND VISITOR ALIKE REMAIN EVER WATCHFUL FOR THIS MOST TENACIOUS OPPORTUNIST.

SCREEEEE

MUIR WOODS

ROADHOGZ TOURS

TOUR BUSES BUILT FOR FLAT, CITY SIGHTSEEING JAUNTS ARE TYING UP THE STEEP ROADS TO **MUIR WOODS**.

RRRRR

BEEP BEEP!

THE TOURIST-LADEN FIVE-TON BEHEMOTHS MUST NAVIGATE THE TWISTING ROADS AT FIVE TO TEN MILES PER HOUR..

...CAUSING LONG LINES OF IRATE DRIVERS.

BEEP!!

BEEP!

REACTION TO COMPLAINTS IS BEST SUMMED UP BY THE OWNER OF **ROADHOGZ TOURS:**

Don't like our driving? Dial T-O-U-G-H L-U-C-K!

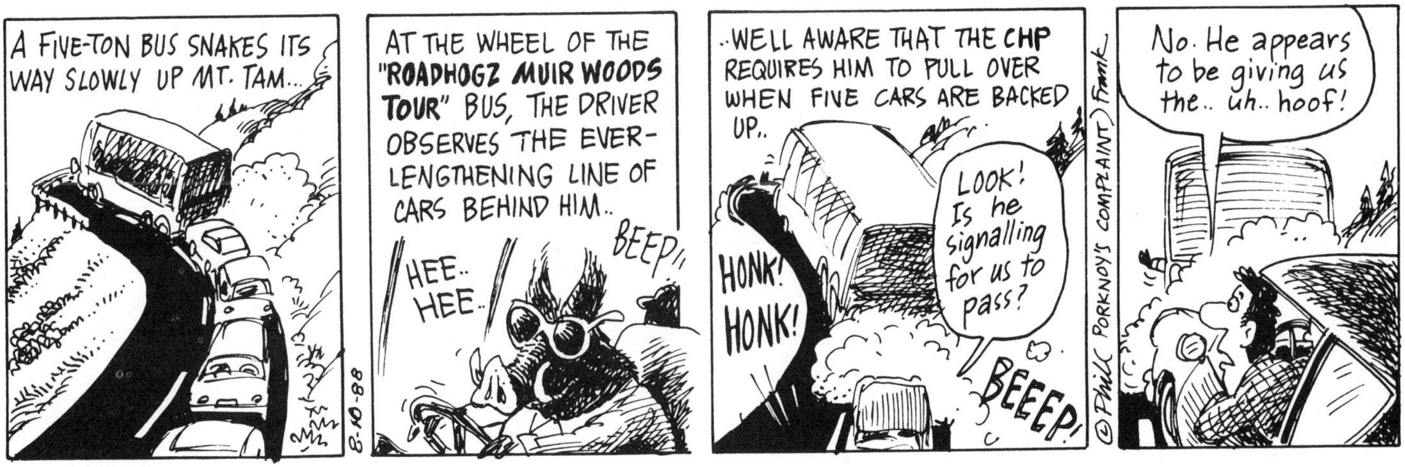
A FIVE-TON BUS SNAKES ITS WAY SLOWLY UP MT. TAM...
8-10-88
AT THE WHEEL OF THE "ROADHOGZ MUIR WOODS TOUR" BUS, THE DRIVER OBSERVES THE EVER-LENGTHENING LINE OF CARS BEHIND HIM..
HEE.. HEE..
BEEP!!
..WELL AWARE THAT THE CHP REQUIRES HIM TO PULL OVER WHEN FIVE CARS ARE BACKED UP..
HONK! HONK!
LOOK! Is he signalling for us to pass?
BEEEP!
© Phil (PORKNOY'S COMPLAINT) Frank
No. He appears to be giving us the.. uh.. hoof!

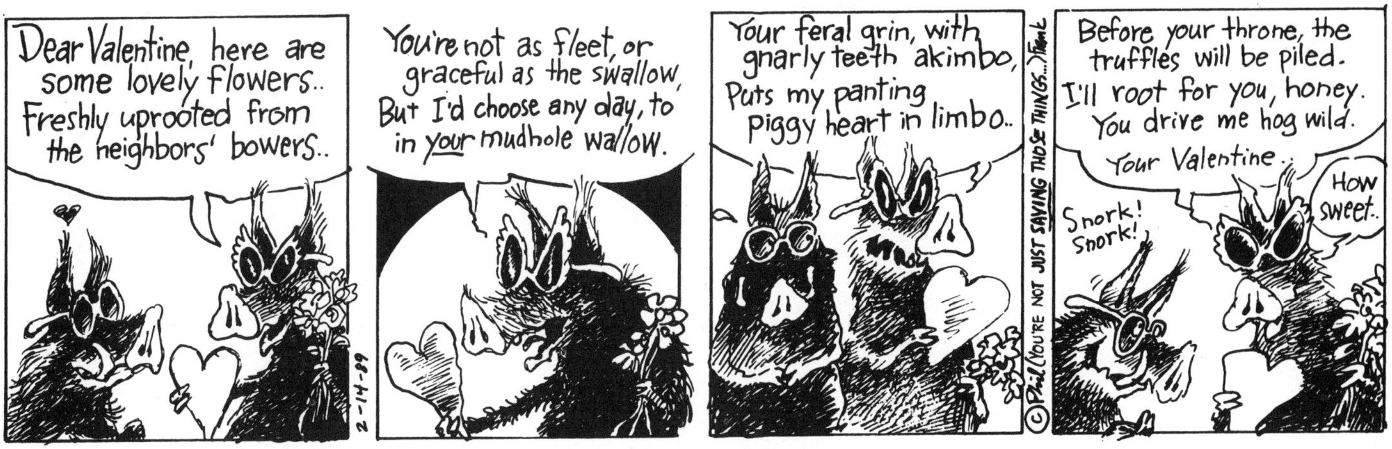
Dear Valentine, here are some lovely flowers.. Freshly uprooted from the neighbors' bowers..
2-14-89
You're not as fleet, or graceful as the swallow, But I'd choose any day, to in your mudhole wallow.
Your feral grin, with gnarly teeth akimbo, Puts my panting piggy heart in limbo..
© Phil (YOU'RE NOT JUST SAYING THOSE THINGS...) Frank
Before your throne, the truffles will be piled. I'll root for you, honey. You drive me hog wild.
Your Valentine..
Snork! Snork!
How sweet..

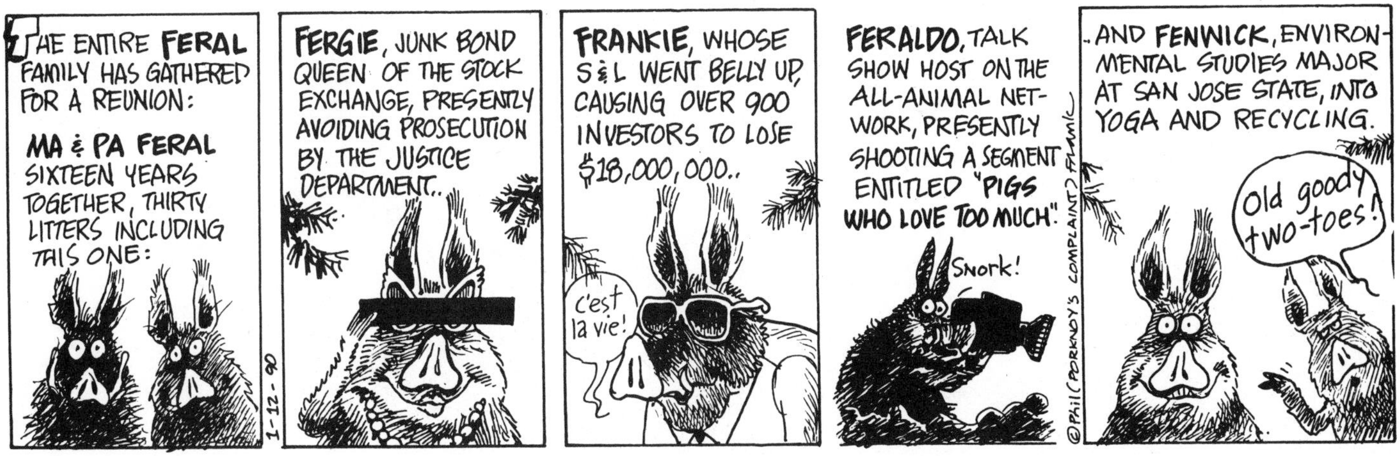
THE ENTIRE FERAL FAMILY HAS GATHERED FOR A REUNION:
MA & PA FERAL SIXTEEN YEARS TOGETHER, THIRTY LITTERS INCLUDING THIS ONE:
1-12-90
FERGIE, JUNK BOND QUEEN OF THE STOCK EXCHANGE, PRESENTLY AVOIDING PROSECUTION BY THE JUSTICE DEPARTMENT..
FRANKIE, WHOSE S&L WENT BELLY UP, CAUSING OVER 900 INVESTORS TO LOSE $18,000,000..
C'est la vie!
FERALDO, TALK SHOW HOST ON THE ALL-ANIMAL NET-WORK, PRESENTLY SHOOTING A SEGMENT ENTITLED "PIGS WHO LOVE TOO MUCH".
Snork!
© Phil (PORKNOY'S COMPLAINT) Frank
..AND FENWICK, ENVIRON-MENTAL STUDIES MAJOR AT SAN JOSE STATE, INTO YOGA AND RECYCLING.
Old goody two-toes!

Who would have the nerve to be the PR flack for Donald Trump in the midst of his messy marriage break up? A feral pig would!

Mr. Trump very much regrets the negative publicity surrounding his pending divorce..

2-20-90

He repeats his strong affection for his wife, Ivana, and his children and prefers that these matters remain private between the two parties. Thank you..

CLICK! CLICK!

© Phil (PASS THE AMMUNITION) Frank

So.. how many times did he visit his new girlfriend at her St. Moritz Hotel room?

Well.. it was worth a shot.

As Mister Trump's spokesman I'd like to reaffirm Donald's hope for an amicable settlement with his wife, Ivana.. Any questions?

2-21-90

Would you clarify his comment about Ivana: "I don't want to create another Leona Helmsley"?

Oh...that. Ahem! Just a silly..

CLICK! CLICK!

How much do you think that statement will anger Ivana?

How much? Well... um... Let's see..

© Phil (GO FORTH AND MULTIPLY) Frank

Say.. 12 million dollars a word.. ..times eight words.. six. Carry the one...

Perhaps you'll explain what Donald Trump meant when he referred to his new girlfriend as.. "much better than a 10!"

Oh, that.. Well, uh..

CLICK! CLICK!

2-22-90

Was he referring to her sexual attractiveness?

Why, heavens no!!

So what was he referring to when he said "She's much better than a 10!"?

Um... her intelligence, no doubt..

© Phil (A MIND IS A TERRIBLE THING..) Frank

You mean her I.Q.?

Help me!! Help me!!

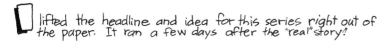

THE CHRONICLE'S EXPOSÉ OF FERAL PIGS WALLOWING IN THE CITY'S RESERVOIRS...

S.F.'s Drinking Water Has Wild Pigs in It

By Jim Doyle
Chronicle Staff Writer

..RESULTS IN A HASTY PRESS CONFERENCE AT THE WATER DEPARTMENT:

8-17-89

I wish to calm the fears of the City's water users. Our drinking water is perfectly safe. We've hired a professional water taster to prove it!

GLUG.. GLUG.. GLUG.. GLUG..

Hmm.. clear and tasty with an interesting earthy bouquet and an aftertaste of...um..

Jimmy Dean Pork Sausage!

CUT!! CUT!!

© Phil (Pork-Noy's Complaint) Frank

As you are aware, we have feral pigs rooting in the City's watershed, polluting the drinking water..

8-19-89

It is our job to do a Swine Damage Survey of the entire 37,000 acre watershed..

These antisocial, unkempt degenerates, have no respect for public property and no social morals..

© Phil (Pork Chop Hill) Frank

In fact, they probably support abortion and flag burning!! These lousy Commie hogs!!

Chief.. uh.. Chief..

A PEEK INSIDE A FERAL PIG ENCAMPMENT IN THE CITY'S WATERSHED:

This is the life, Fred. We should summer here every year.

SNORK!

SNORK!

8-18-89

I'm going to forage under the trees...

While you're at it, be a doll and root me up a tuber.

I want to work on my tan..

© Phil (The Baste is Yet to Come) Frank

Be careful! I smell bacon frying.

NOT FUNNY, FRED!

THE SWINE DAMAGE SURVEY IS UNDERWAY IN THE CITY'S WATERSHED:

I can't believe it! ..Tromping through the woods lookin' for **wild pigs**!

I got _enough_ things to do in my life without havin' to keep track of a bunch of hairy hogs.. ..fact is.. I don't even think they..

8-20-89

..they.. ..HOLY PORK RINDS!!

© Phil PORK-LIPS NOW!! Frank

Hey, Sweet Potato Pie.. did you hear a noise just now?

Relax, my honey-baked ham. It's just the wind.

THE SWINE DAMAGE SURVEY IS UNDERWAY IN THE CITY'S WATERSHED:

This is Jackson. I'm in sector four, north end of the Calaveras Reservoir...

Go ahead, Jackson.

Hey, man! I got about 400 pounds of the best-lookin' ribs and pork sausage sunnin' itself fifty yards from me. Over.

Move in and confront them! Over.

8-21-89

San Francisco Water Department! You're trespassing on City property!

??

You're only allowed in here if you have one of these badges..

BADGES, BADGES? WE DON'T GOT TO SHOW YOU NO STEENKING BADGES!!

© Phil LINKS TO THE PAST. Frank

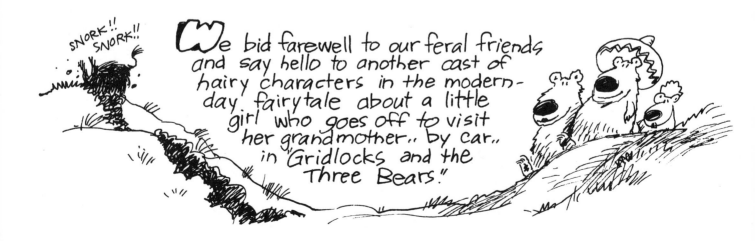

SNORK!! SNORK!!

We bid farewell to our feral friends and say hello to another cast of hairy characters in the modern-day fairytale about a little girl who goes off to visit her grandmother.. by car.. in "Gridlocks and the Three Bears."

"Gridlocks and the Three Bears"

Once upon a time in the not too distant future, an independent little girl named "Gridlocks" decides to drive from her Piedmont condo to visit her Grandmother's apartment in the City.

I'll leave as soon as I finish my cappuccino, Grams...

GRIDLOCKS HOPS INTO HER LITTLE RED SPORTS CAR AND ZIPS THROUGH THE PASTORAL LANDSCAPE OF THE EAST BAY HILLS..

10-20-87

VROOOM

SHE MERGES ONTO HIGHWAY 24 AND SUDDENLY HER CAR IS ENGULFED BY A SHADOW.. A SCARY BEAST? A STORM?.. ..OR **WORSE**?

OH, NO!! AN AC TRANSIT BUS!!

©Phil (MASSED TRANSIT) Frank

Hi, Grams...I'm going to be a little late... ..like a **day** late..

GRIDLOCKS and the 3 BEARS

As GRIDLOCKS INCHES HER WAY THROUGH TRAFFIC, TOWARDS HER GRANDMOTHER'S HOUSE IN THE CITY, SHE FACES MANY PERILS..

CARPOOL

..INCLUDING PERSONAL GUILT..

SHAME ON YOU, GRIDLOCKS!! YOU SELFISH LITTLE BRAT!!

??

YOU SHOULD BE CARPOOLING... LIKE US!! WE'RE GOING TO GET YOU!!

©Phil (AGAINST ALL O2) Frank

.. AND YOUR LITTLE DOG, TOO!!

Great! I don't even **have** a dog!

GRIDLOCKS and the THREE BEARS

SO FAR.. GRIDLOCKS, ON HER WAY TO GRANDMA'S HOUSE, HAS BEEN RUN OFF THE ROAD BY A NOT-SO-FRIENDLY WOODSMAN..

NACHO
-BUZZ OFF!!

10-22-87

..ACCOSTED BY HIGHWAYMEN...

SLOW
MEN WORKING

...CHASED BY A FIRE-BREATHING MONSTER..

HOOONK!

©Phil (COMMUTE MY SENTENCE) Frank

...AND IMPRISONED AT THE BAY BRIDGE TOLL PLAZA.

Next fairy tale this girl's going to go visit grandma on Bart...

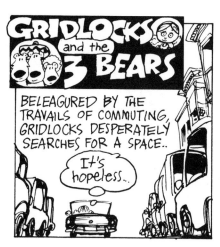

GRIDLOCKS and the 3 BEARS

BELEAGUERED BY THE TRAVAILS OF COMMUTING, GRIDLOCKS DESPERATELY SEARCHES FOR A SPACE..

It's hopeless..

I know!! The magic ring Grandma gave me!!

AS GRIDLOCKS RUBS THE MAGIC RING, TRAFFIC BUILDS BEHIND HER..

Parking Fairy.. Parking Fairy are.. wherever you are Give me a place To park my car!

POOF

SUDDENLY... AT THE CORNER OF GRANT AND COLUMBUS...

WOW! I'M IMPRESSED!

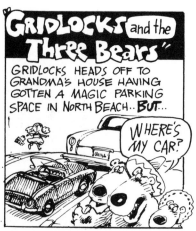

GRIDLOCKS and the Three Bears"

GRIDLOCKS HEADS OFF TO GRANDMA'S HOUSE HAVING GOTTEN A MAGIC PARKING SPACE IN NORTH BEACH.. BUT...

WHERE'S MY CAR?

"SOMEBODY'S PARKED IN MY SPACE!!" SAID PAPA BEAR..

TWENTY-TWO YEARS I'VE PARKED IN THIS VERY SPOT!

This fairy tale needs to be rewritten! Give me the magic phone!!

LATER.. GRIDLOCKS RETURNS:

MY CAR!! It's gone! What happened, Mr. Frog?

Honey.. you've been (HEE, HEE) TOAD! Where's my kiss?

The name's Gridlocks Gr...r...i...d...

RIBIT!

BBRRRRRRRR..

Bolinas.. the little West Marin town that just wanted to be left alone, that didn't desire visitors and went out of its way to discourage tourists, was cutting down directional road signs. Bolinas finds itself the focus of attention when Mayor Feinstein, who had granted sister-city status to 11 international cities, decided to confer the status on Bolinas as well.

THE YEAR IS 2088. IN THE STRATOSPHERE HIGH ABOVE PLANET EARTH A LARGE TABLET TUMBLES IN ORBIT..

..IS IT A SPACE PROBE CARRYING KNOWLEDGE TO DISTANT REACHES OF THE COSMOS?..

„OR..: DOES IT CARRY A MESSAGE FOR VISITORS FROM OTHER GALAXIES?

ONLY CALTRANS KNOWS FOR SURE.

CALTRANS SERVICE MODULE 326 INSTALLS A DIRECTIONAL MARKER HIGH ABOVE THE EARTH'S SURFACE. THE YEAR IS 2088.

We got 'em **this** time!

Roger, Sir..

THE NEWLY INSTALLED MARKER IS LEFT TO TUMBLE LAZILY IN ORBIT..

„DIRECTING INTERPLANETARY TOURISTS TO THE QUAINT SEASIDE...

...VILLAGE OF... OOPS! SPOKE TOO SOON!

This is Bolinas Border Patrol. We have the sign in sight. Over.

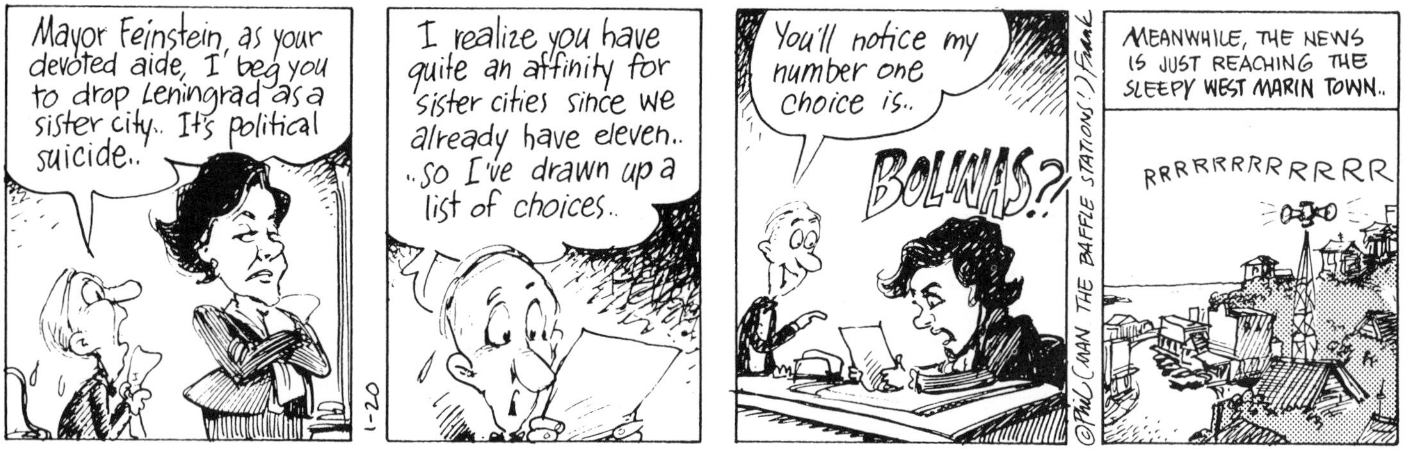
Mayor Feinstein, as your devoted aide, I beg you to drop Leningrad as a sister city.. It's political suicide..
1-20
I realize you have quite an affinity for sister cities since we already have eleven.. ..so I've drawn up a list of choices..
You'll notice my number one choice is..
BOLINAS?!
©Phil (MAN THE BAFFLE STATIONS!) Frank
MEANWHILE, THE NEWS IS JUST REACHING THE SLEEPY WEST MARIN TOWN..
RRRRRRRRRRRRR

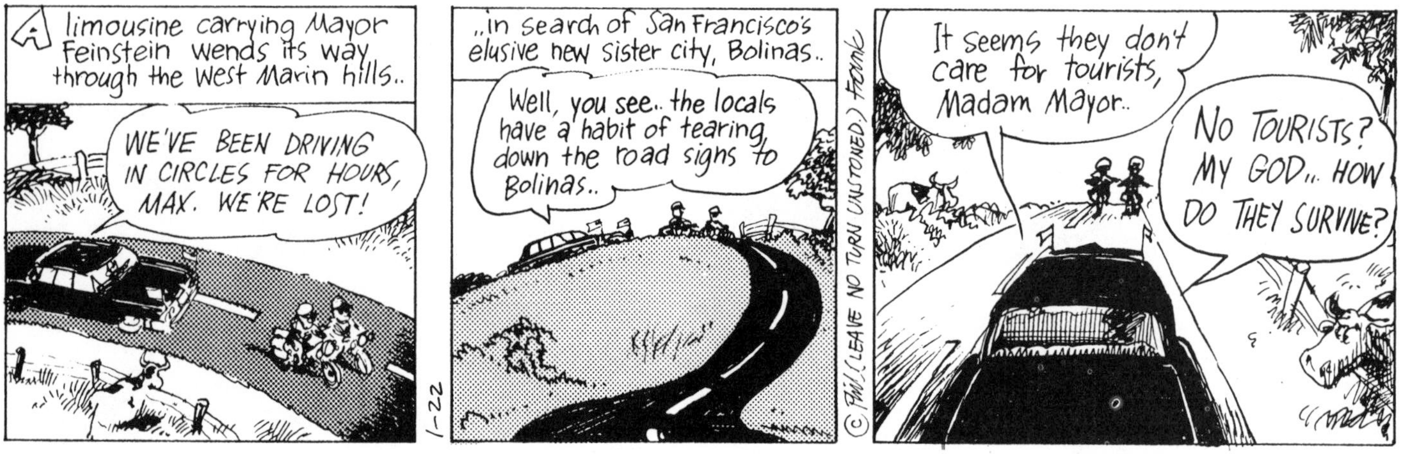
A limousine carrying Mayor Feinstein wends its way through the West Marin hills..
WE'VE BEEN DRIVING IN CIRCLES FOR HOURS, MAX. WE'RE LOST!
1-22
..in search of San Francisco's elusive new sister city, Bolinas..
Well, you see.. the locals have a habit of tearing down the road signs to Bolinas..
©Phil (LEAVE NO TURN UNSTONED) Frank
It seems they don't care for tourists, Madam Mayor..
NO TOURISTS? MY GOD.. HOW DO THEY SURVIVE?

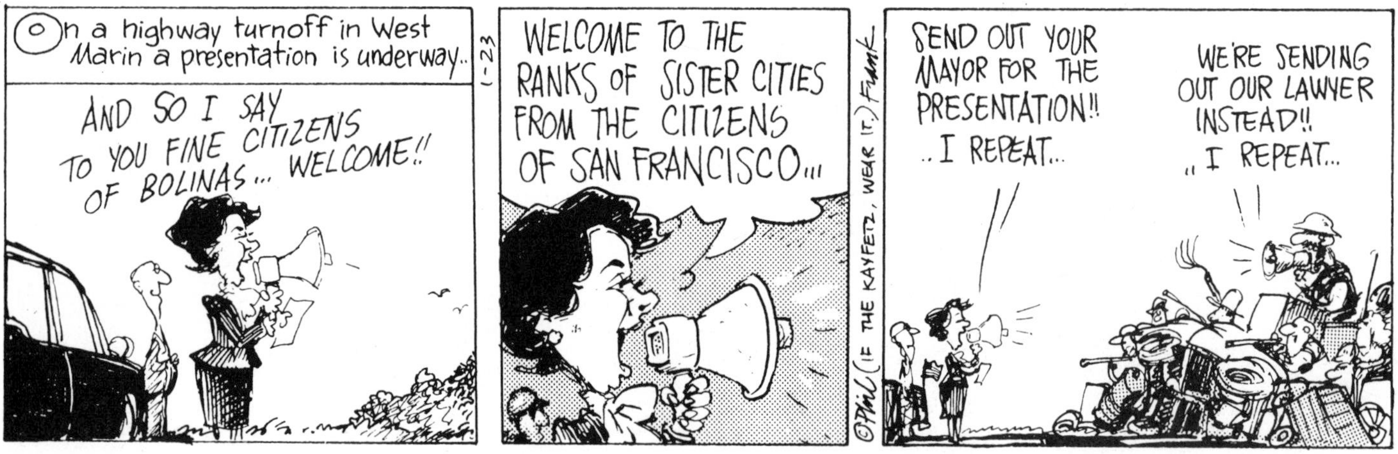
On a highway turnoff in West Marin a presentation is underway..
AND SO I SAY TO YOU FINE CITIZENS OF BOLINAS... WELCOME!!
1-23
WELCOME TO THE RANKS OF SISTER CITIES FROM THE CITIZENS OF SAN FRANCISCO...
©Phil (IF THE KAYFETZ, WEAR IT.) Frank
SEND OUT YOUR MAYOR FOR THE PRESENTATION!! ..I REPEAT...
WE'RE SENDING OUT OUR LAWYER INSTEAD!! ..I REPEAT...

And so it is with great honor, citizens of Bolinas, that I bestow upon you the honored title of Sister City of San Francisco!!

"And toss this symbolic key to the city over your barricade. Welcome, friends!!

As the attorney for the aforementioned parties I must point out a technicality.. We're a town, not a city... Here's your key back!

1-24

Start the limo, Max. I'll toss it over again, and we'll split before they can throw it back.

Got it.

PLINK!

©Phil Cone Last Fling, Frank

Meanwhile, back at the ranch...

Chief...I've finished that story about the 86-year-old grandmother being attacked by monster cockroaches...

Cancel it!... **and** this 'rampaging rhino at the zoo' story..

But...

2-5-88

Instead I want you to do a story about massage and its deep-rooted ties to oriental philosophy..

EDITOR

Amazing what a difference putting decaf in the coffee machine can make..

©Phil Calm me in the morning, Frank

AVERY WORDWRIGHT, MANAGING EDITOR OF THE **DAILY REQUIREMENT** IS STUMPED:

Hmm.. emigrating Russians are buying houses in the City's Sunset district..

It's a good story that needs just the right headline..

Who could come up with it?

FARLEY!!

Yes?

6-20-90

THE NEXT MORNING:

Daily Requirement
RED SALES IN THE SUNSET

©Phil (somewhere over the rainspout) Frank

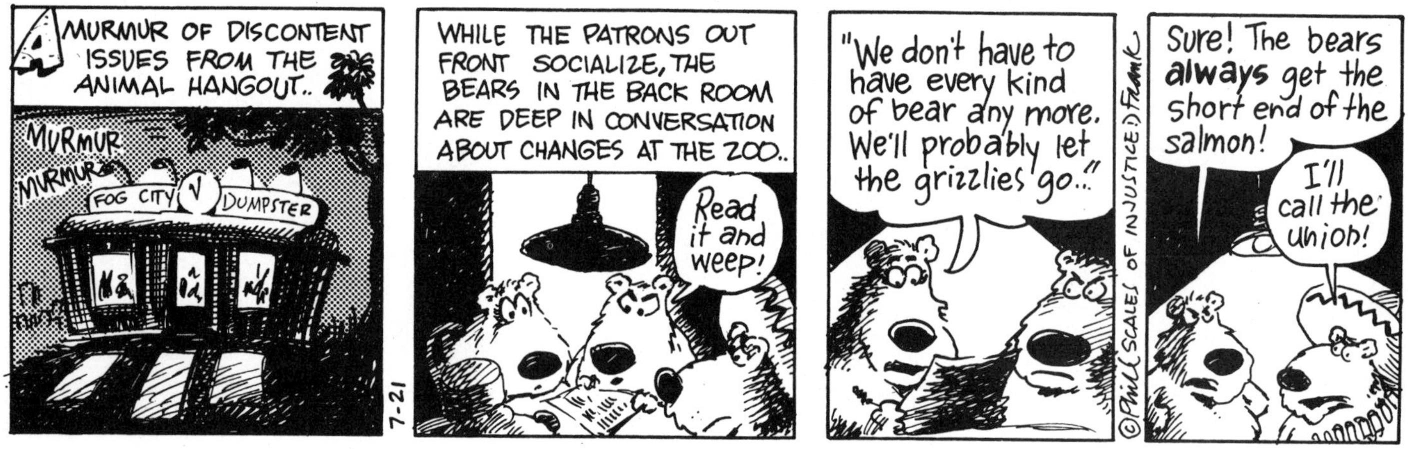
A MURMUR OF DISCONTENT ISSUES FROM THE ANIMAL HANGOUT..
MURMUR
MURMUR
FOG CITY DUMPSTER
7-21
WHILE THE PATRONS OUT FRONT SOCIALIZE, THE BEARS IN THE BACK ROOM ARE DEEP IN CONVERSATION ABOUT CHANGES AT THE ZOO..
Read it and weep!
"We don't have to have every kind of bear any more. We'll probably let the grizzlies go.."
© Phil (SCALES OF INJUSTICE) Frank
Sure! The bears **always** get the short end of the salmon!
I'll call the union!

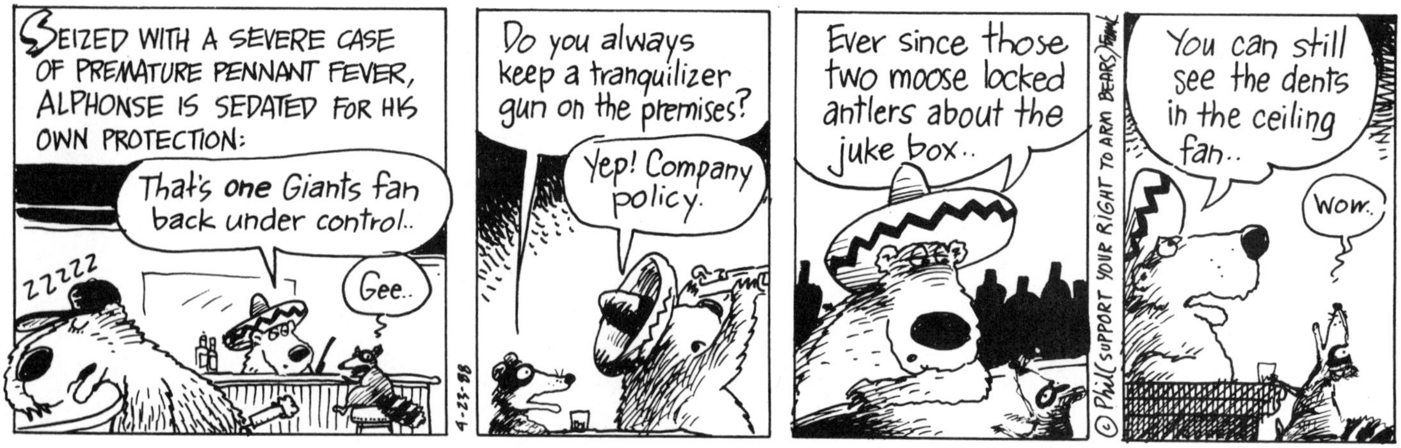
SEIZED WITH A SEVERE CASE OF PREMATURE PENNANT FEVER, ALPHONSE IS SEDATED FOR HIS OWN PROTECTION:
That's **one** Giants fan back under control..
ZZZZZ
Gee..
4-25-88
Do you always keep a tranquilizer gun on the premises?
Yep! Company policy.
Ever since those two moose locked antlers about the juke box..
© Phil (SUPPORT YOUR RIGHT TO ARM BEARS) Frank
You can still see the dents in the ceiling fan..
Wow..

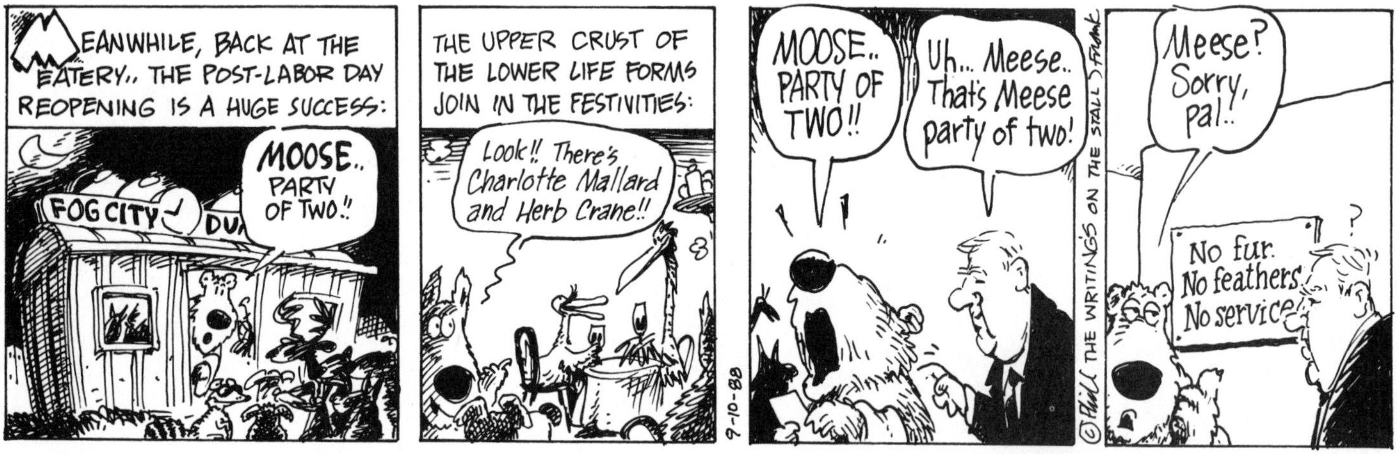
MEANWHILE, BACK AT THE EATERY.. THE POST-LABOR DAY REOPENING IS A HUGE SUCCESS:
FOG CITY DU
MOOSE.. PARTY OF TWO!!
THE UPPER CRUST OF THE LOWER LIFE FORMS JOIN IN THE FESTIVITIES:
Look!! There's Charlotte Mallard and Herb Crane!!
9-10-88
MOOSE.. PARTY OF TWO!!
Uh... Meese.. That's Meese party of two!
© Phil (THE WRITINGS ON THE STALL) Frank
Meese? Sorry, pal..
No fur. No feathers. No service.

THERE'S TROUBLE AFOOT AT THE **FOG CITY DUMPSTER**:

City Health Inspector..

(Gulp.) I don't suppose you're here for lunch..

Just a routine inspection of your kitch.. **YOW!**

Uh.. That's our chef..

This is a flagrant violation of health codes!! He must be wearing a hair net..

A hair net?

NO HAIR NET.. NO LICENSE! I'LL BE BACK TOMORROW!

But..

It's a body stocking, Victor. Please?

Only in San Francisco.

© Phil (VICTOR'S SECRET) Frank

HILDA CHECKS OUT THE CUSTOMERS AT THE BAR OF THE **FOG CITY DUMPSTER**:

Hi, boys. New in town?

Yeah... we just hopped in...

Where you fellows from?

The Angels Camp frog jumping contest..

Hey! You're a couple of those African Goliath frogs that were going to wipe out the locals..

Don't remind us..

(Sigh!)

Too bad about Sports Illustrated scrubbing the cover photo..

Next she's going to ask us about the steroid allegations..

BARTENDER! TWO MORE!

© Phil (IT'S NOT EASY BEING GREEN) Frank

THE TWO **AFRICAN GOLIATH FROGS**, JUST ARRIVED FROM **ANGELS CAMP**, LUNCH AT THE **FOG CITY**:

WAITER!!

Look at my soup! What do you see in it?

um.... a fly..

A FLY! YES.. A FLY! **ONE** LOUSY FLY! YOU SHOULD BE ASHAMED TO PUT FLY SOUP ON YOUR MENU!

I'll be right back.

I saw one go through here a minute ago..

They're never around when you want them.

© Phil (CAPTAIN CUISINE) Frank

Steve Silver of "Beach Blanket" fame is hired to do the musical introduction for the 1988 Oscars Show. He camps it up, putting Sleeping Beauty in a mini skirt, singing a lusty song. Disney gets upset, threatens to sue.

When people ask me why I went local I point to stories like this and say... see!! see!! It's as if people are writing my material for me. The Evil Queen on the witness stand? I couldn't wait!!

Row 1

THE **DISNEY VS. STEVE SILVER** TRIAL CONTINUES:

Your honor.. it is the intention of the defense to prove that **Snow White** is a woman of many moods.. not just the few dictated by Disney Studios..

Call your first witness.

Where were you on the night of March 29th last, Mr...uh.. Bashful?

Well.. I was watching the Oscars show on T.V. I took a particular interest in the portrayal of Snow White..

4-11-89

Are you suggesting that the character of Snow White as a mini-skirted rock singer was a mis-representation?

Heck no! It just reminded me of some of the great parties we had at the cabin..

©PHIL (JUST A BABE IN THE WOODS) FRANK

OBJECTION!!

ALL RIGHT!!

BANG!! BANG!!

Row 2

THE DEFENSE IN THE **DISNEY VS. STEVE SILVER** TRIAL CALLS A WITNESS:

The defense calls the Evil Queen.

GASP!

4-12-89

How would you describe your relationship with Snow White..

That of a devoted and loving step-mother..

BOOO!! HISSSS!!

ORDER IN THE COURT!!

Did you not order the 'Huntsman' to take her out to the woods?

Remember.. You're under oath..

Well...

If I'd heard that Creedence Clearwater album one more time I'd have...

OBJECTION!

©PHIL (A ROYAL PAIN) FRANK

Row 3

THE PROSECUTION IN THE **DISNEY VS. STEVE SILVER** TRIAL QUESTIONS SNOW WHITE'S STEPMOTHER, THE EVIL QUEEN:

Did you not find Snow White to be a virtuous woman?

4-13-89

Well, she **did** set up housekeeping in a cabin with seven lonely bachelors...

Because **you** forced her to hide for her life in fear of your jealousy!!

Your honor, I contend that Snow White was a victim of this woman..

..Just as Steve Silver victimized her in his copyright-infringing portrayal of her.!!

©PHIL (NOT A MAN TO BE TRUFFLED WITH) FRANK

How do you plan to make _that_ connection?

The prosecution calls Prince Charming.!!

THE DEFENSE IN THE **DISNEY VS. STEVE SILVER** TRIAL CALLS A WITNESS: 4-14-89

So, Prince.. tell the court in your own words what it was like living with Ms. White..

Well.. I don't know that "happily ever after" would describe our relationship..

We had a lot of trouble communicating.. We tried marriage counselors, family therapists.. ..you name it.. but that "princess" attitude of hers...

Am I to understand that you eventually divorced?

She took me to the royal cleaners..

© Phil (WASH AND SMEAR) Frank

THE JUDGE IN THE **DISNEY VS. STEVE SILVER** TRIAL HANDS DOWN HER RULING: 4-15-89

I find the defendant, Steve Silver to be **not guilty** of copyright infringement..

But..

To the prosecution I say.. Parody and satire are protected by the First Amendment...

But..

And to Mr. Silver... ..Have you ever knowingly reproduced the likeness of Mickey or Minnie Mouse?

Yes, your honor..

But..

Good. I want you to make me a big hat for the Black & White Ball with Mickey and Minnie Mouse..

Yes, your honor..

But..

© Phil (THE BROTHER GRIN) Frank

Hi-ho... hi-ho... it's home from court we go...

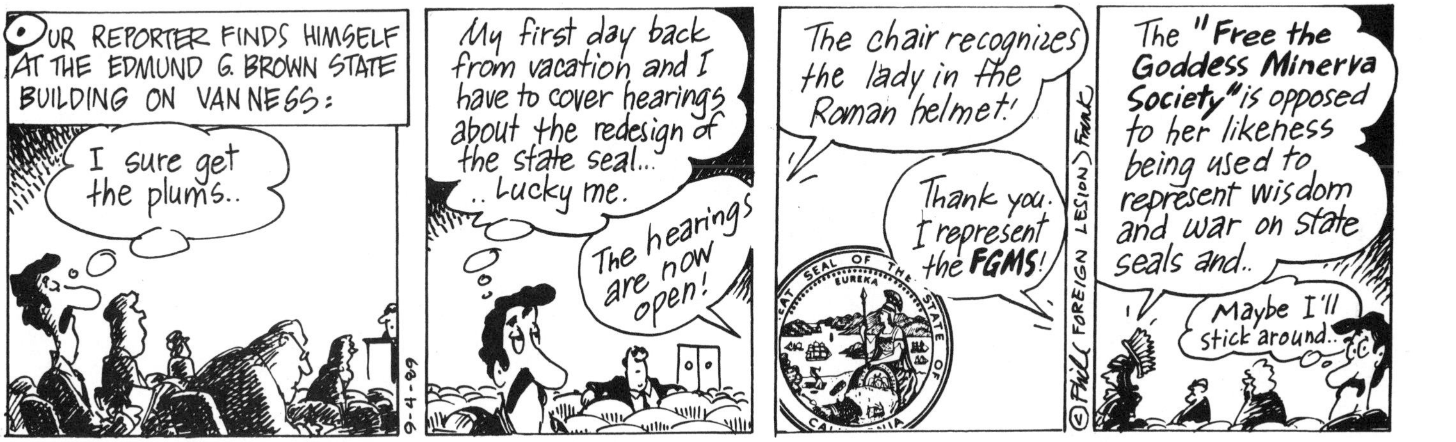
OUR REPORTER FINDS HIMSELF AT THE EDMUND G. BROWN STATE BUILDING ON VAN NESS:
I sure get the plums..
9-4-89
My first day back from vacation and I have to cover hearings about the redesign of the state seal... ..Lucky me.
The hearings are now open!
The chair recognizes the lady in the Roman helmet!
THE GREAT SEAL OF THE STATE OF CALIFORNIA
EUREKA
Thank you. I represent the FGMS!
© Phil (FOREIGN LESION) Frank
The "Free the Goddess Minerva Society" is opposed to her likeness being used to represent wisdom and war on state seals and..
Maybe I'll stick around..

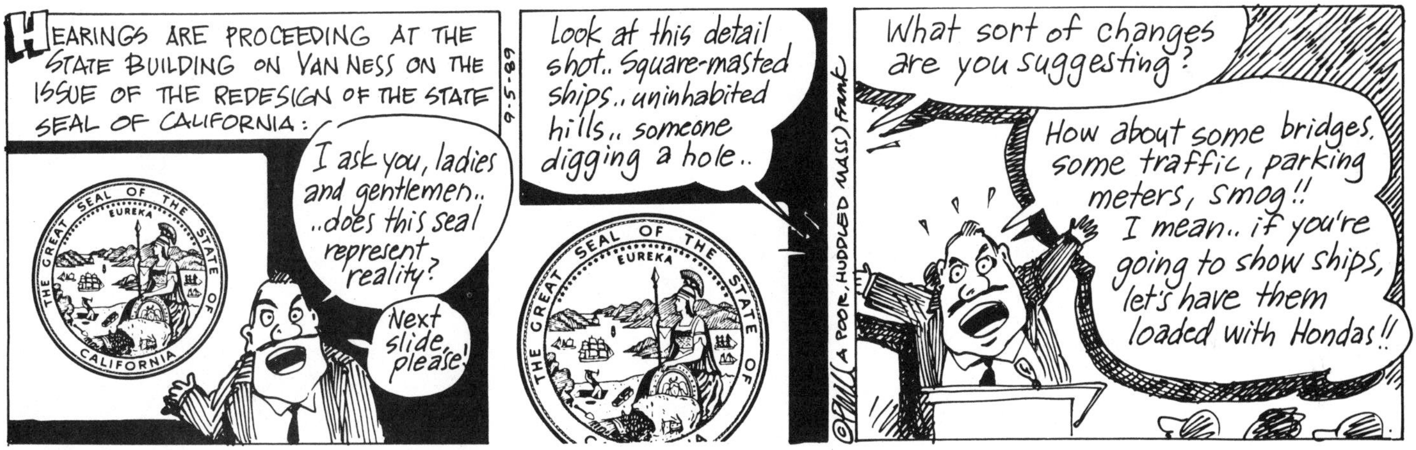
HEARINGS ARE PROCEEDING AT THE STATE BUILDING ON VAN NESS ON THE ISSUE OF THE REDESIGN OF THE STATE SEAL OF CALIFORNIA:
9-5-89
THE GREAT SEAL OF THE STATE OF CALIFORNIA
EUREKA
I ask you, ladies and gentlemen.. ..does this seal represent reality?
Next slide, please!
Look at this detail shot.. Square-masted ships.. uninhabited hills.. someone digging a hole..
© Phil (A POOR, HUDDLED MASS) Frank
What sort of changes are you suggesting?
How about some bridges, some traffic, parking meters, smog!! I mean.. if you're going to show ships, let's have them loaded with Hondas!!

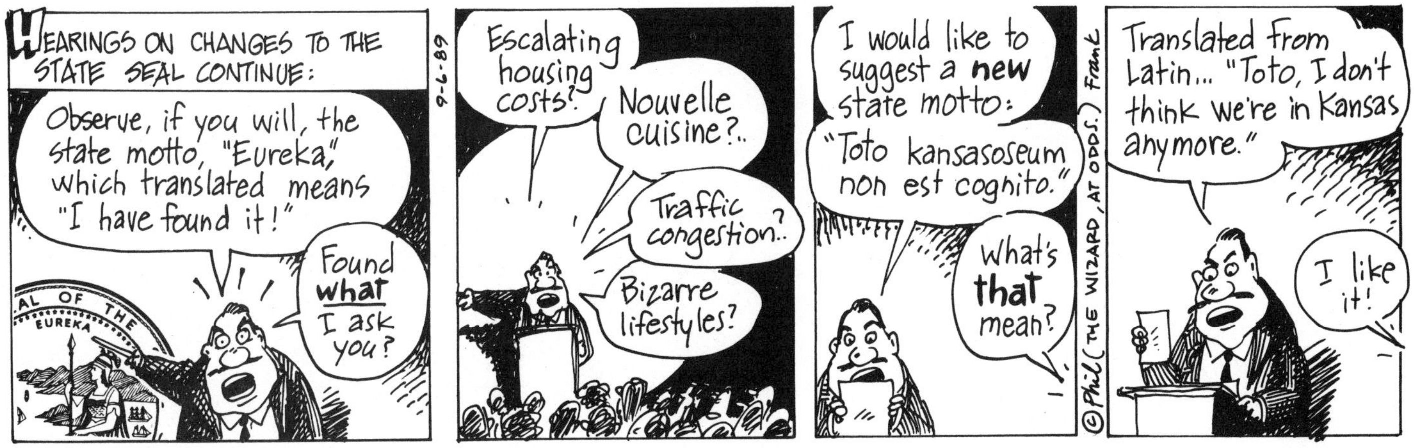
HEARINGS ON CHANGES TO THE STATE SEAL CONTINUE:
9-6-89
Observe, if you will, the state motto, "Eureka," which translated means "I have found it!"
Found what I ask you?
EUREKA
Escalating housing costs?
Nouvelle cuisine?..
Traffic congestion?..
Bizarre lifestyles?
I would like to suggest a new state motto: "Toto kansasoseum non est cognito."
What's that mean?
© Phil (THE WIZARD, AT ODDS.) Frank
Translated from Latin... "Toto, I don't think we're in Kansas anymore."
I like it!

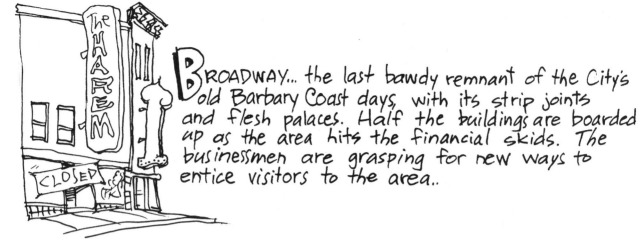

BROADWAY... the last bawdy remnant of the City's old Barbary Coast days, with its strip joints and flesh palaces. Half the buildings are boarded up as the area hits the financial skids. The businessmen are grasping for new ways to entice visitors to the area..

Owners of the North Beach topless clubs are meeting in the basement of **El Seed**.. Al, owner of the **House of Flesh**, addresses the group.

Gentlemen..

Business is way off for us.. Clearly we have a problem..

We must adapt to changing morals or we'll drown. With this in mind I have called in an advisor from one of the smartest mobs on the coast..

You don't mean?...

Yes.. Stanford.

Gentlemen.. allow me to introduce sexual psychologist, Prof. L. Gordon Penwipper.

CLAP!! CLAP!! CLAP!

Professor Penwipper, sexual psychologist from Stanford, addresses a meeting of Broadway club owners..

Gentlemen.. I perceive your problem thusly..

Your decreased revenues are a direct result of changing social mores.. Voyeurism and common sexuality no longer arouse the American public..

We must redefine what is erotic in the human mind.

For example..

GASP!

LIVE! ON STAGE!! Monogamous Couples in Therapy!!

Stanford sex psychologist Professor L. Gordon Penwipper proposes a way to revitalize the sex industry on Broadway..

So you see, gentlemen.. Americans today are turned on by money, security, image.

LIVE! ON STAGE MONOGAMOUS COUPLES IN THERAPY!

2-12

Professor.. I have an idea but it may be too sordid...

Don't be shy..

©Phil (YUP, YUP AND AWAY.) FRANK

"TALK TO A FULLY-CLOTHED WOMAN ABOUT YOUR **IRA**!"

Why not? Let's pull out all the stops..

LIVE!

ACTION!

There always seems to be a movie being filmed on the streets of the City... so it seemed like a subject ripe for comment. I needed a movie to parody and "**Never Cry Wolf**" had just been released and was getting lots of press. I put the Fog City crew to work filming "**Never Cry Bear**."

ONE OF MANY MOVIE COMPANIES IS ON LOCATION IN SAN FRANCISCO FOR THE FILMING OF "**NEVER CRY BEAR**."

SILENCIO!! ROLLING! ACTION!!

"NEVER CRY BEAR," the sensitive portrayal of an animal scientist...

(played by Bruin Hilda)

6-9

...who leaves the solitude of her wooded homeland to study the wildlife of the urban jungle..

ZOOM!

WELCOM TO SAN FRANC

©PHIL BRUTE FARCE) FRANK

..so that she and her kind might learn of the ways of the human species..

The Remington Micro screen shaves you close all over.

1299

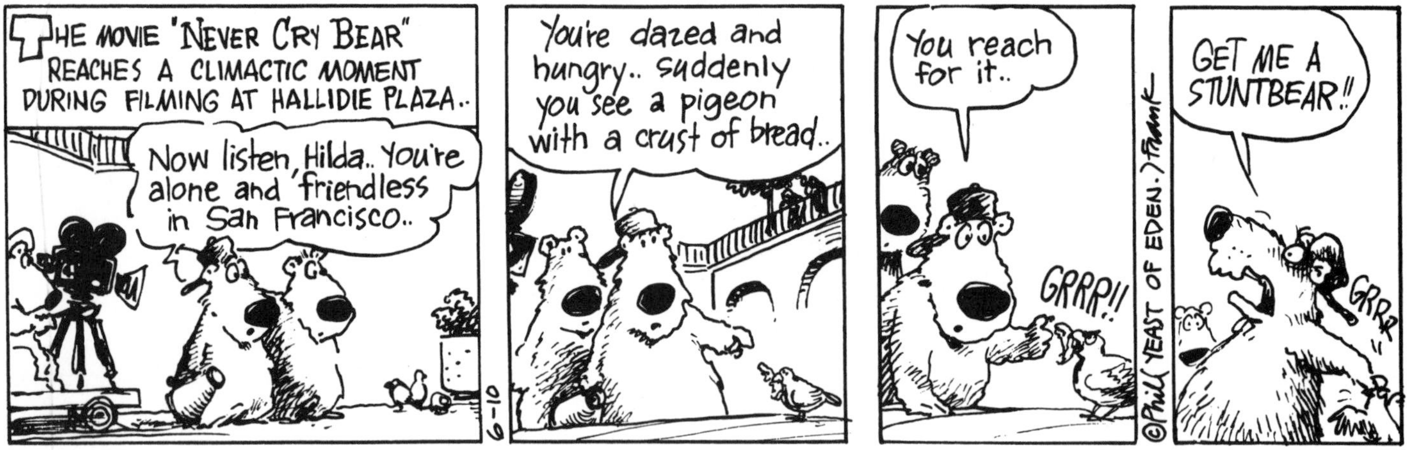
THE MOVIE "NEVER CRY BEAR" REACHES A CLIMACTIC MOMENT DURING FILMING AT HALLIDIE PLAZA..
Now listen, Hilda.. You're alone and friendless in San Francisco..
You're dazed and hungry.. suddenly you see a pigeon with a crust of bread..
6-10
You reach for it..
GRRR!!
©Phil (YEAST OF EDEN.) Frank
GET ME A STUNTBEAR!!
GRRR

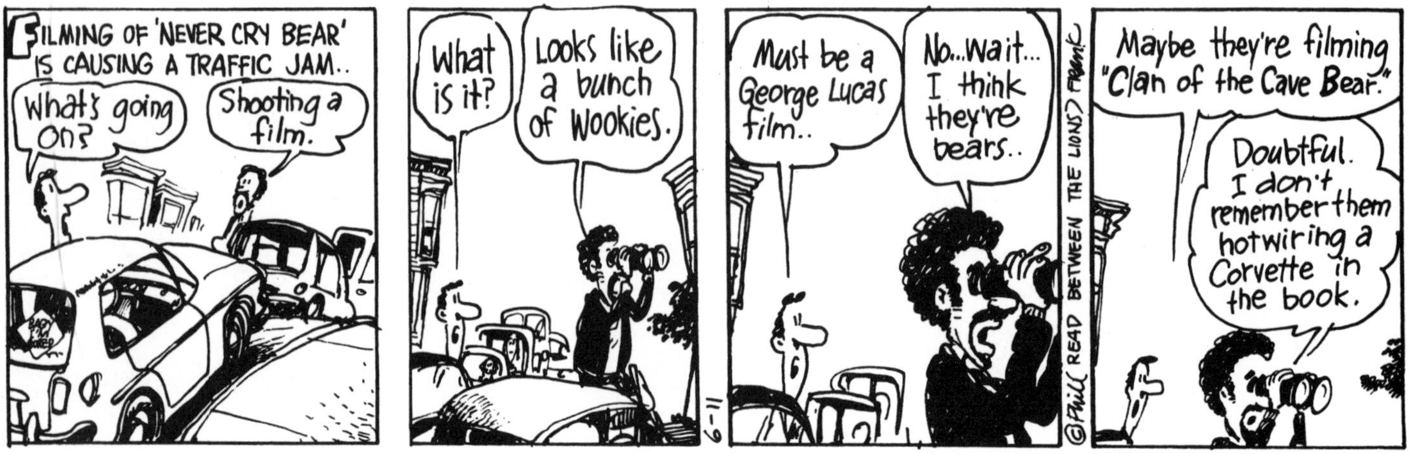
FILMING OF 'NEVER CRY BEAR' IS CAUSING A TRAFFIC JAM..
What's going on?
Shooting a film.
What is it?
Looks like a bunch of Wookies.
6-11
Must be a George Lucas film..
No...wait... I think they're bears..
©Phil (READ BETWEEN THE LIONS) Frank
Maybe they're filming "Clan of the Cave Bear."
Doubtful. I don't remember them hotwiring a Corvette in the book.

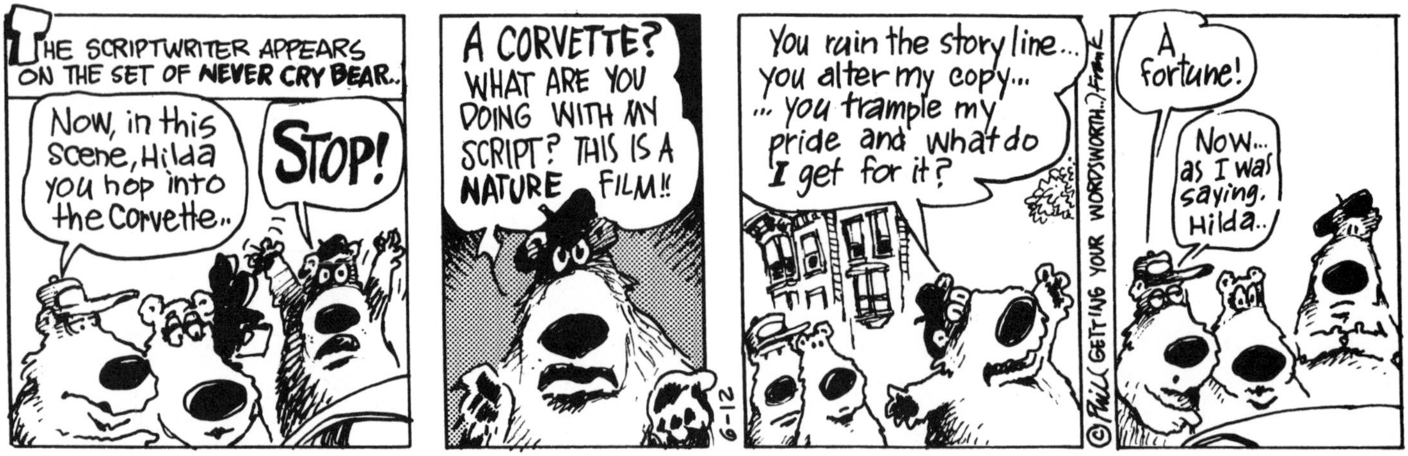
THE SCRIPTWRITER APPEARS ON THE SET OF NEVER CRY BEAR..
Now, in this scene, Hilda you hop into the Corvette..
STOP!
A CORVETTE? WHAT ARE YOU DOING WITH MY SCRIPT? THIS IS A NATURE FILM!!
6-12
You ruin the story line... you alter my copy... ... you trample my pride and what do I get for it?
©Phil (GETTING YOUR WORDSWORTH..) Frank
A fortune!
Now... as I was saying, Hilda..

Panel 1: BEAVER STREET IN THE CASTRO DISTRICT IS CLOSED OFF FOR A LOCATION SHOT FOR THE FILM "NEVER CRY BEAR"...

Now in this scene, Hilda..

Panel 2: You are befriended by a human animal even though you have been taught to be wary of these creatures..

Panel 3: He is calm and quiet. Suddenly his animal instincts and rage surface..

Why?

6-13

Panel 4: Because this Datsun grabs his parking space.

©Phil (INVADERS FROM OUTER RICHMOND) Frank

Panel 5: "NEVER CRY BEAR", THE TOUCHING STORY OF AN ANIMAL SCIENTIST STUDYING HOMO SAPIENS IN HIS NATURAL HABITAT, IS BEING SHOT IN SAN FRANCISCO.

PERFECTO! CUT!!
CLICK!!

10-3

Panel 6: ..BUT POOR FINANCING, GREED, RUMORS OF DRUGS ON THE SET AND PETTY SQUABBLING ON TOP OF A BAD SCRIPT UNDERMINE MORALE...

This film stinks!
Tell me about it!

Panel 7: ..AND *NOW*, THE TEAM OF WRITERS MEETS TO CONSIDER A CHANGE OF TITLE — ALWAYS A SIGN OF PROBLEMS..

We need a title with the ring of success..
©Phil (BAD NEWS, BEARS) Frank

Panel 8: How about "HOWARD THE BEAR"?
ARE YOU CRAZY?

Panel 9: THINGS ARE NOT GOING WELL ON THE SET OF "NEVER CRY BEAR" PRESENTLY ON LOCATION IN A *SOMA* EATERY.

SILENCIO!!

10-4

Panel 10: RUMORS OF CASH FLOW PROBLEMS ADD FUEL TO THE PETTY BICKERING AMONG THE CAST...

He's an insensitive, brutish beast!
But... He's a BEAR!

Panel 11: AND UNFORSEEN PROBLEMS ARISE..

WE'RE BEING PICKETED? BY WHOM?
Sierra Club and Friends of Animals..
PINK FLOYD
©Phil (THE FURRY WITH THE SINGE ON TOP) Frank

Panel 12: Oh, No!
THIS MOVIE USES REAL FURS!
ANIMALS ARE PEOPLE TOO!

Ever since Alcatraz was decommissioned as a Federal prison in 1963, its future had been in limbo. It was designated as a national park in 1972, a part of the Golden Gate National Recreation Area. But still, ideas for other uses for the island were proposed... The most recent scheme being that it be turned into an off-shore casino.

NEWS THAT ALCATRAZ MIGHT BE TURNED INTO A CASINO COMPELS PASSENGERS ON A RENO-BOUND BUS TO PAY THE ISLAND A QUICK VISIT...

Hey, Smokey!! Which of these is the $5 window?

?

Love this Slot!! *Every* time I put in a quarter it pays off!!

STAMPS

HEY!! What do you get when you line up three oranges?

Three cans of orange soda.

©Phil C (PEEL OF FORTUNE) Frank

THE NEWS THAT ALCATRAZ MIGHT BECOME A CASINO HAS REACHED AREA GAMBLERS. THEY FLOCK TO THE ISLAND..

Well.. we're certainly pleased to see so many local visitors..

Most people are unaware that Alcatraz is a rookery for many sea birds...

©Phil C (IS IT A BOY OR A GULL?) Frank

What do you think the chances are of this baby gull surviving to adulthood?

Ten to one says he doesn't make it!

You're on!

I'll take five bucks of that action!

What's the point spread?

Side bets? Side bets anyone?

FARMS IN BERKELEY? GAMBLING ON ALCATRAZ? THE CURIOUS COME TO TOUR..

This is the cell of the infamous "Longshot" Scampi, the 1920's racketeer.

He was convicted of various swindles.. ..bilking poor people in numbers games.. ..rigging lotteries and slot machines..

How ironic! Now the government's thinking of doing the same thing with this place.

They say that when the moon is full a sardonic laugh is heard from this very cell

Амернка прекрасное Место!

The Russian bears are coming!! Promotion materials arrived indicating that the Moscow Circus was scheduled to play San Francisco. The most popular part of the show had always been the performing bears. Maybe they have relatives in the U.S. that they can visit while in the States. Getting the Russian translations correct was complicated but worth the effort.

Alphonse! You've got a post card from some relatives in Russia.

Uncle Knopa and Aunt Tisha?

"Hello and kind greetings to American nephew, Alphonse. Aunt Tisha and I are still with Moscow Circus, soon to be in your city. Please to allow us to stay with most generous relative.

THE FINEST TRAINED BEAR ACT IN THE WORLD!!

"There are now eleven bears in our act...

Also the largest trained bear act in the world..

"Seeing you soon, Uncle Knopa"

I suppose we could stamp it "HIBERNATING" and send it back.

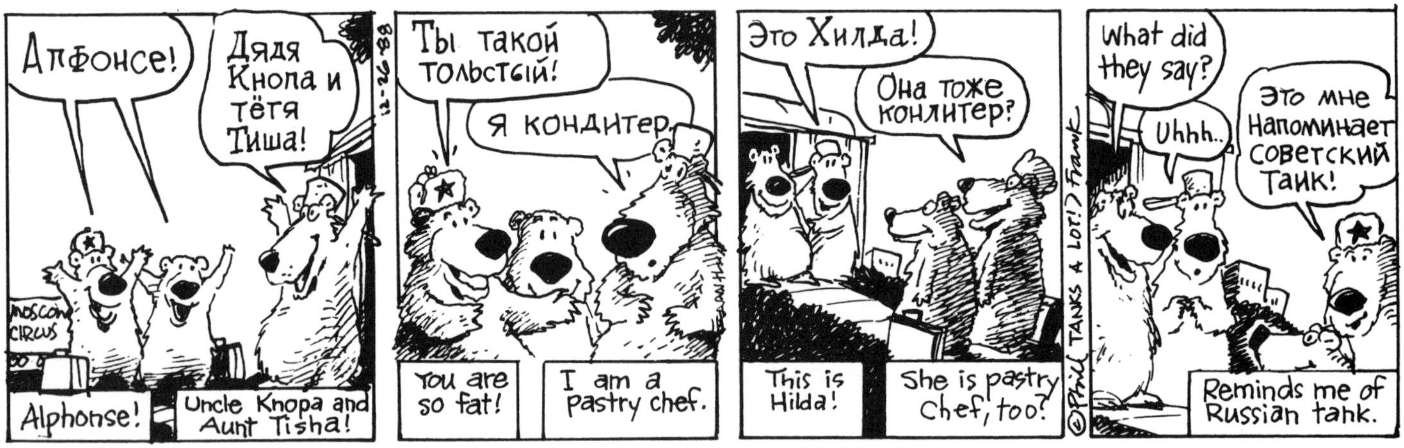

12-26-88
Апфонсе!
Дядя Кнопа и тётя Тиша!
Alphonse!
Uncle Knopa and Aunt Tisha!
Ты такой тольстый!
Я кондитер.
You are so fat!
I am a pastry chef.
Это Хилда!
Она тоже конлитер?
This is Hilda!
She is pastry chef, too?
What did they say?
Uhhh..
Это мне напоминает советский танк!
Reminds me of Russian tank.
© Phil (TANKS A LOT!) Frank

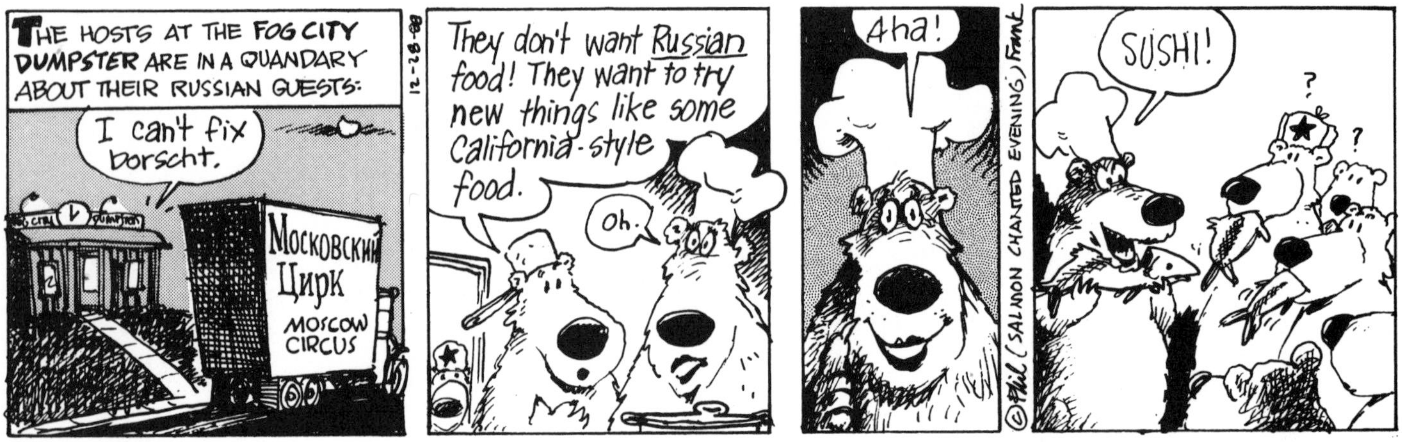

THE HOSTS AT THE FOG CITY DUMPSTER ARE IN A QUANDARY ABOUT THEIR RUSSIAN GUESTS:
I can't fix borscht.
Московский Цирк
MOSCOW CIRCUS
12-28-88
They don't want Russian food! They want to try new things like some California-style food.
Oh.
Aha!
SUSHI!
?
?
© Phil (SALMON CHANTED EVENING) Frank

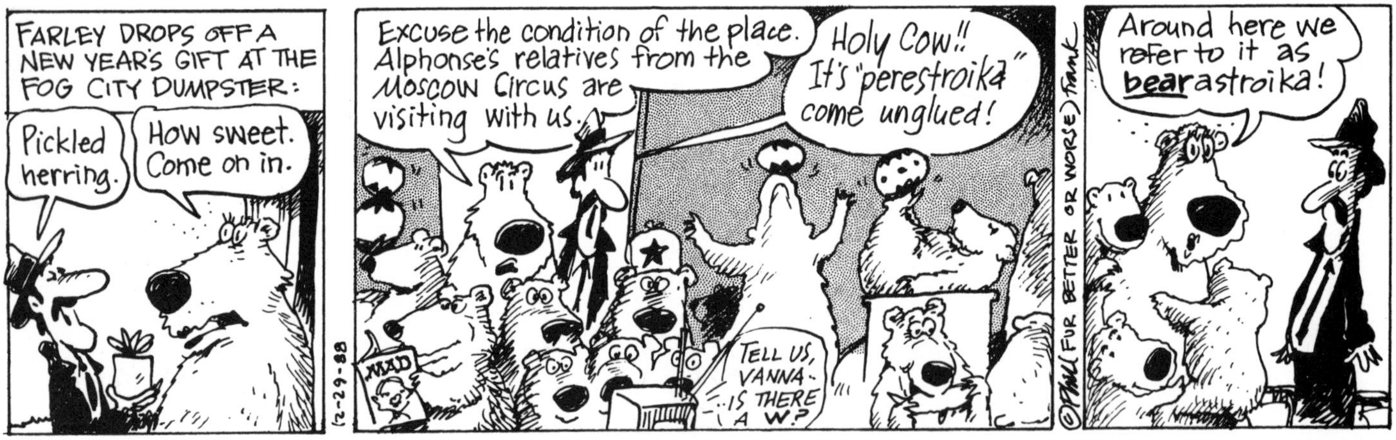

FARLEY DROPS OFF A NEW YEAR'S GIFT AT THE FOG CITY DUMPSTER:
Pickled herring.
How sweet. Come on in.
12-29-88
Excuse the condition of the place. Alphonse's relatives from the Moscow Circus are visiting with us.
Holy Cow!! It's "perestroika" come unglued!
MAD
TELL US, VANNA - IS THERE A W?
Around here we refer to it as bearastroika!
© Phil (FUR BETTER OR WORSE) Frank

THE BEARS FROM THE MOSCOW CIRCUS ENJOY THE SIGHTS:

DING!
DING!

Что ты хочешь видеть, дядя?

what would you like to see, uncle?

Мэжкл Джэксон, Тина Тёрнер, Чикагские Медведи.

Почему Чикагские Медведи?

Michael Jackson, Tina Turner and the Chicago Bears.

Why the Chicago Bears?

Русские медведи могут джонглировать, но Чикагские Медведи играют футбол и выигрывают!

Russian bears can juggle, but Chicago Bears can play football... and **win!**

THE ENTIRE MOSCOW CIRCUS BEAR TROUPE AND THEIR AMERICAN RELATIVE TOUR THE CITY:

WHEN SUDDENLY THEY ARE SURROUNDED BY THE CITY'S FINEST.

RRRRRR

RRRR

A DISCUSSION ENSUES:

We have some foreign nationals declaring diplomatic immunity from the City's leash law. Can they do that?

Убегайте!

Run for it!

CIAO!!

CIAO!!

Московский Цирк

Art Agnos is elected to take the reins at City Hall.

THE EDITORIAL CARTOONIST AT THE DAILY REQUIREMENT TRIES OUT HIS LATEST CARICATURE ON A REPORTER.

Well.. what do you think?

Let's see...

12-9-87

Ted Kennedy?

NO...

Gorbachev?

NO!!

Lee Iacocca?

NO!! NO!! It's our new mayor!

Gee... I'm sorry..

It's okay, Farley... Our politicos all have Wonderbread faces... How I miss Quentin Kopp..

©Phil (WRINKLE RESISTANT) Frank

Agnos' face has no lines... no furrows..

Don't worry.. ..a few months at City Hall should fix that.

PAT.. PAT..

ART! ART! Where are you?

A new mayor arrives on the scene, swept into office on a wave of grass-roots neighborhood support. While he is experienced in many areas of politics, he appears weak in the area of "working the press". In a switch on the government leak to the press via "Deep Throat" in the Watergate scandal, Farley is sent in as "Deep Hat" by his editor. His job is to advise Mayor Art on how to give good press.

Farley.. The readers are on our backs about our hounding of Mayor Agnos..

4-11-88

But Art isn't giving us what we need for good copy. The man doesn't know how to use the press. He needs to be educated.

Getting my drift?

You want me to do something, don't you?

©Phil (BACK ME UP, SCOTTY) Frank

The media has come full circle. Now we want to leak information to the government..

Hmm.. like Watergate with a backflush. Good concept, chief.

Here's what you're to do.. set up a meeting with the mayor... Give him some inside dope on how to get good press.

Okay..

EDITOR

4-12-88

Be careful.

Do I have a code name?

From now on you're "DEEP HAT"!

Got it, Chief..

And wear this to protect your identity!

No wonder undercover work is so risky.. you can't **see** anything..

© Phil (CLOAK AND STAGGER) Frank

"DEEP HAT" MAKES HIS INITIAL CONTACT WITH THE MAYOR..

Hello, Art.. ..I have some very useful information for you..

4-13-88

Say... who **is** this?

Let's just say I'm a friend.

© Phil (NIGHT OF THE "ROUND TABLE") Frank

Meet me in the Civic Center garage tomorrow night at nine, near the west stairs..

Why would I ever agree to something like that?

Wouldn't you like to know how Dianne got such good press?

Hey, I'll **be** there. Should I bring a pizza or something?

THE MAYOR ENTERS THE CIVIC CENTER GARAGE FOR HIS MEETING WITH "**DEEP HAT**", HIS MEDIA INFORMANT..

Psst! Art! Over here!

4-14-88

I have friends who have some information for you.. You would like to get the kind of press coverage Dianne got, wouldn't you?

Yes.. Yes!! How did she do it?

It was as if there were **four** Feinsteins.. ..She was everywhere getting press every day!!

Art.. Art.. ..Art..

© Phil (THE QUAD SQUAD) Frank

There **were** four of them..

THAT'S HOW SHE DID IT! I **KNEW** IT!!

"DEEP HAT," THE **DAILY REQUIREMENT'S** TOP UNDERCOVER REPORTER, IS LEAKING INFORMATION TO THE MAYOR:

I can't believe what you're saying.. that there were **four** Dianne Feinsteins..

How else do you think she got so much press?

But.. how can you prove that?

Would a photograph convince you?

Why... That's the "**Washbag**"... with **FOUR** Dianne Feinsteins at the entrance.!!

A near fatal slip in scheduling..

I WANT THAT PHOTO!

So does she, Art.. ..so does she..

"DEEP HAT" AND THE MAYOR MOVE THEIR CONSULTATIONS TO AN OBSCURE CHINESE RESTAURANT:

I don't know how to thank you for your advice..

That's okay, Art.

We want to see you succeed as mayor. Remember.. ..sometimes quick, decisive action is called for.

Believe me, I've learned my lesson about **that**.

Would you care to order?

Hmm..uh..let's see.. Could I get back to you on that... say.. um. Tuesday?

Art... Art..

THE BOARD OF SUPERVISORS MEETS AT CITY HALL:

Our agenda today deals with ways to cut the City's $150 million deficit.

Any ideas?

Yes.. We could save a quarter of a million dollars by not increasing our salaries like we've planned..

Moving right along..

Hey! Do we really need ambulances?

You won't believe the cuts they're making in the City budget. Listen in on line two...

THIS IS **911**.. IF YOU WISH TO REPORT A CRIME.. PRESS 1. ..FOR FIRE.. PRESS 2..

..FOR A CRIME **DURING** A FIRE... PRESS 3. IF YOUR BUSINESS IS ON FIRE.. PRESS 4. IF YOUR HOME IS ON FIRE... PRESS 5..

IF **YOU** ARE ON FIRE ENTER YOUR SOCIAL SECURITY NUMBER...... NOW.

© PHiL (NO! NO! I SAID A BUD LITE!) Frank

THE NEWS THAT SEVERAL SAN FRANCISCO BRANCH LIBRARIES WILL BE CLOSING CREATES A NEW 'ILLICIT INDUSTRY:

Psst! Hey, kid... ..c'mere. I want to show you something..

Here. Look at this. It's for you.

TREASURE ISLAND?!! Gosh! Thanks, mister.

In case you want to buy any more, you know where to come.

YOU BET! I'll tell all my friends!

© Phil Booked for life. Frank

Hee, hee... ..The first one's always free..

OUR REPORTER STANDS ON GREEN STREET AND STARES AT THE SPOT WHERE HE LAST SAW HIS CAR.

Sigh..

Well... life goes on.. even when you don't have a set of wheels..

I know! I'll do something that I haven't done in years! I'll ride the cable car to work!

© Phil RIDE ON THE WILD SIDE Frank

San Francisco Chronicle

The Largest Daily Circulation in Northern California

TOURISTS THROW S.F. RESIDENT OFF CABLE CAR

"He Had a Lot of Nerve Getting on a Ride Built For Us!"
Omaha Visitor

VICTIM OF ATTACK

The big news in the art world in 1988 was the arrival here of the Andrew Wyeth exhibit **"The Helga Pictures"**. The subject seemed ripe for lampooning because of all the fawning going on over the pieces. I went through the exhibit and procured a transcript of the audio tour. From that **"The Hilda Pictures"** emerged. The Achenbach Foundation for Graphic Arts requested and received the originals.

WITH ONLY TWO WEEKS LEFT.. CROWDS POUR IN TO SEE THE DE YOUNG'S LATEST EXHIBIT..

..IT IS A COLLECTION OF WATERCOLORS, TEMPERAS, DRYBRUSH AND PENCIL DRAWINGS BY ANDREW WYETH, ONE OF AMERICA'S BEST-KNOWN PAINTERS...

..THEY DETAIL HIS FIFTEEN-YEAR RELATIONSHIP WITH A MOST UNUSUAL FEMALE MODEL.

WELCOME TO...

The Hilda Pictures

© PUT OUT ON A LIMB/Frank

"THE HILDA PICTURES" EXHIBIT AT THE DE YOUNG IS GRACED BY A SURPRISE VISITOR—THE STAR OF THE SHOW.

Gee, Hilda..

I had **no idea** you had this 15-year-long relationship as a model for Andrew Wyeth..

There's a lot you don't know about me.

This seems to be everyone's favorite portrait. It's called **"Braids"**

Gosh.. you wore your fur long in those days.

Well, it **was** the 1960's...

© PHIL/HERE TODAY, GONE TOMORROW/Frank

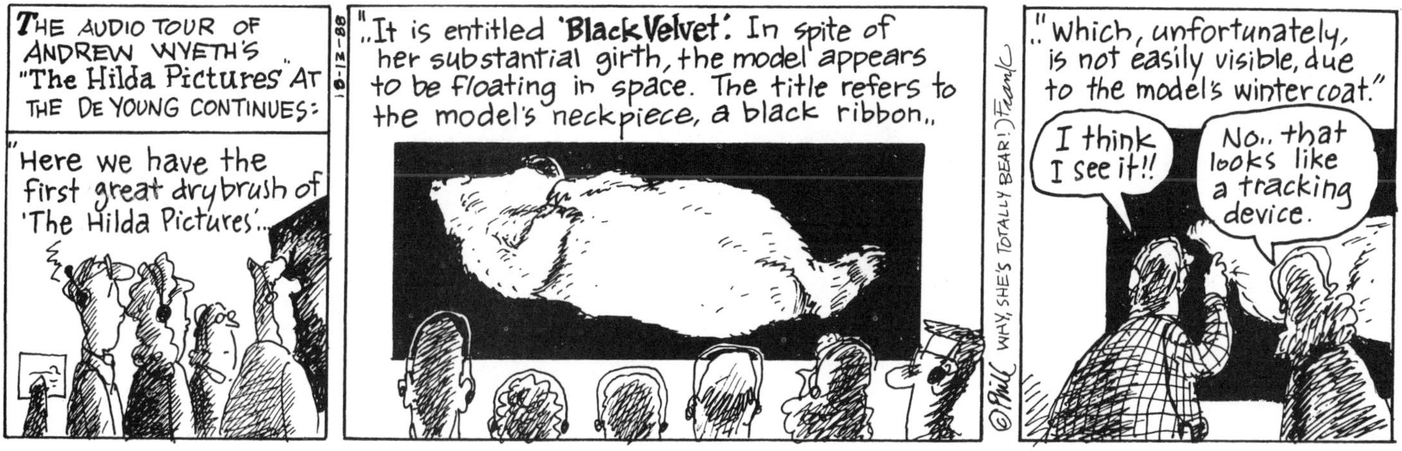
THE AUDIO TOUR OF ANDREW WYETH'S "The Hilda Pictures" AT THE DE YOUNG CONTINUES:
"Here we have the first great drybrush of 'The Hilda Pictures'...
"..It is entitled 'Black Velvet.' In spite of her substantial girth, the model appears to be floating in space. The title refers to the model's neckpiece, a black ribbon..
".. Which, unfortunately, is not easily visible, due to the model's winter coat."
I think I see it!!
No.. that looks like a tracking device.
10-13-88
©Phil (WHY, SHE'S TOTALLY BEAR!) Frank

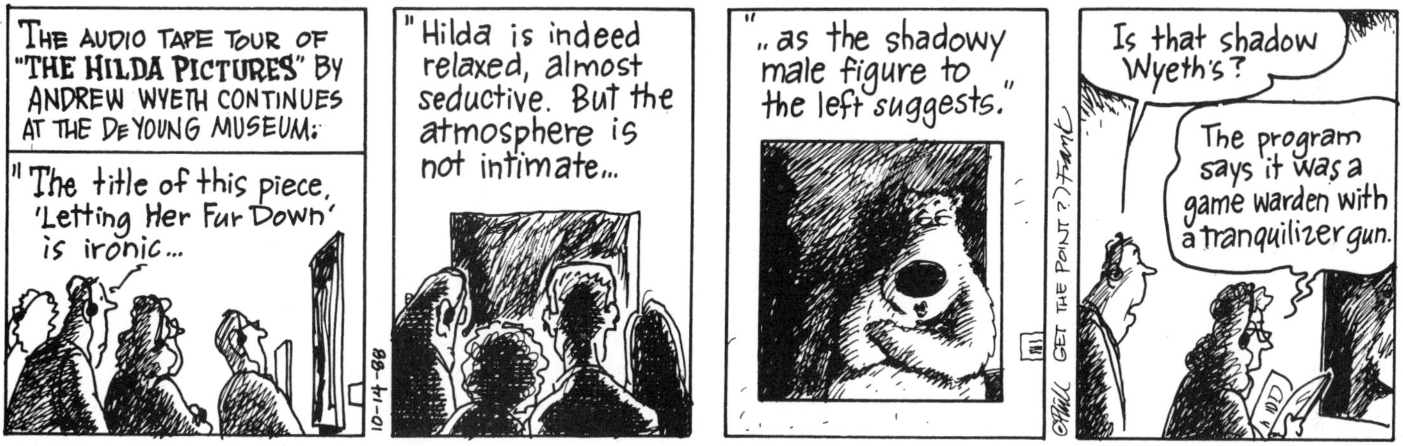
THE AUDIO TAPE TOUR OF "THE HILDA PICTURES" BY ANDREW WYETH CONTINUES AT THE DE YOUNG MUSEUM:
"The title of this piece, 'Letting Her Fur Down' is ironic...
"Hilda is indeed relaxed, almost seductive. But the atmosphere is not intimate...
".. as the shadowy male figure to the left suggests."
Is that shadow Wyeth's?
The program says it was a game warden with a tranquilizer gun.
10-14-88
©Phil (GET THE POINT?) Frank

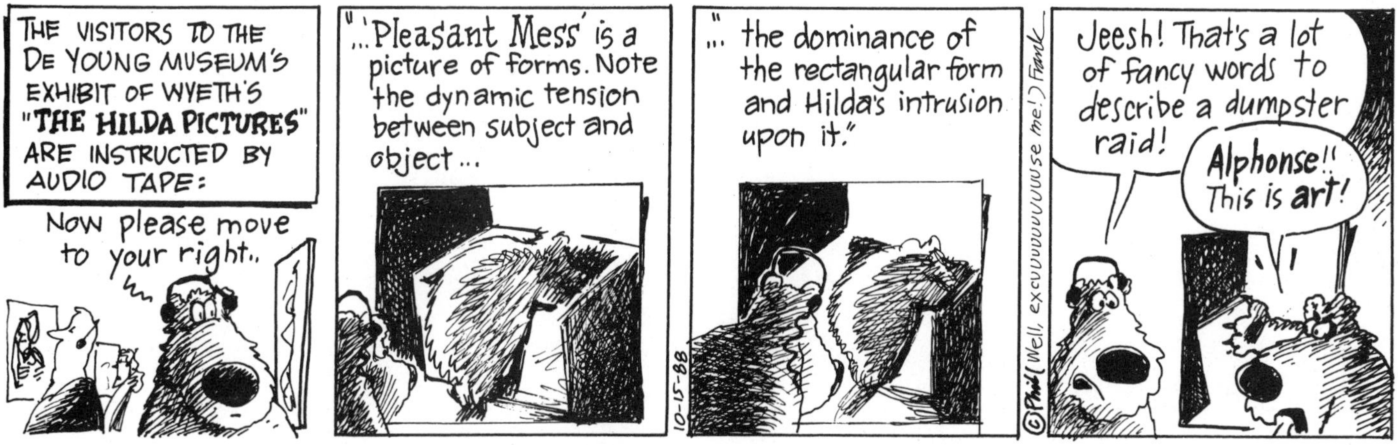
THE VISITORS TO THE DE YOUNG MUSEUM'S EXHIBIT OF WYETH'S "THE HILDA PICTURES" ARE INSTRUCTED BY AUDIO TAPE:
Now please move to your right..
"...'Pleasant Mess' is a picture of forms. Note the dynamic tension between subject and object...
"... the dominance of the rectangular form and Hilda's intrusion upon it."
Jeesh! That's a lot of fancy words to describe a dumpster raid!
Alphonse!! This is art!
10-15-88
©Phil (Well, excuuuuuuuuuse me!) Frank

WELCOME TO CROCKETT
Future Home of the **U.S.S. MISSOURI?**

The U.S.S. Missouri, loved and despised by many, and the focus of nuclear activists concerns was a recurring story in local news as its future home port was being argued. Who would offer the Missouri a home? A letter to the editor in the Chronicle from a resident in Crockett suggested their local Sea Scouts dock. How could I resist?

SOMEWHERE IN THE PACIFIC ON THE U.S.S. MISSOURI:

Now hear this!! This is the Captain speaking. We are receiving results of the latest voters poll in San Francisco...

A majority of voters strongly support the homeporting there of the Missouri...

YEAH!!

However... They don't want to pay for the dredging..

BOOOOOOO

However!! Mitsubishi will pay for dredging in exchange for installing Ty advertising monitors on the foredeck and in all turrets.. ? ? ? ?

FURTHER RESULTS OF THE MOST RECENT POLL OF VOTERS IS BROADCAST TO ALL HANDS ABOARD THE MISSOURI:

San Franciscans who favor the Missouri but not nuclear weapons... ...22%!

San Franciscans who favor the Missouri and nuclear weapons but simply can't abide the color gray.... 14%...

San Franciscans who favor the Missouri and nuclear weapons and the color gray but who think **63** is an unlucky number... 12%..

and finally, San Franciscans opposed in principle to anything whatsoever... 52%!

THE OFFICERS IN CHARGE OF NAVAL DEPLOYMENT GATHER FOR A SECRET MEETING..

Gentlemen..

The future home porting of the battleship Missouri has taken a dramatic turn!

GASP!

San Francisco, our first choice, has not exactly welcomed us with open arms... but I hold here a letter of invitation..

From Art Agnos?

No.. it's from a resident of the town of Crockett..

Dear sirs,...

©Phil (A NOVEL ENGAGEMENT) Frank

WHERE SAN FRANCISCO HAS TURNED ITS BACK ON THE U.S.S. MISSOURI, ANOTHER CITY HAS SPREAD ITS WELCOMING ARMS:

Sure! Bring it to Crockett!

ALREADY, PREPARATIONS ARE UNDERWAY. A BERTH HAS BEEN RESERVED...
...ALONGSIDE THE SEA SCOUTS DOCK...

I wouldn't tie up there if I were you.

..THEY'RE GEARING UP AT THE OUTBOARD MOTOR SHOP..

Yeah.. say.. do you have any handbooks on nuclear-powered outboards?

©Phil (IN SEARCH OF THE GOLDEN FLEETS) Frank

.. AND SPECIALTY ITEMS ARE GOING ON SALE AT THE HARDWARE STORE.

MILITARY HAMMERS
$97.00 EACH!
TAKE YOUR PICK!

A LETTER OF INVITATION FROM A CROCKETT RESIDENT TO THE U.S.S. MISSOURI HAS BROUGHT A RESEARCH TEAM FROM THE NAVY..

I like it!!

Look.. it's got great water access, housing, transportation, friendly locals..

...and there's even the element of security..

Security?

It took us an hour and a half to find the place.. think of how long it would take the Russkis!

©Phil (FROM RUSSIA WITH... DIRECTIONS) Frank

"PRESIDIO"

...The Dance of the Dying Military Base:

With the news out of Washington that the Presidio army base would be shut down as part of a military cost-cutting program, an amazing comic opera began unfolding with many players, including the liberal representatives, Barbara Boxer and Nancy Pelosi, so I related the story **as** a comic opera with accurate Italian lyrics and song titles..

"PRESIDIO" The Dance of a Dying Military Base. The curtain rises on the hero, General Quarters, as he receives the news of his base's closing.

1-9-89

From the 8th hole of the golf course he sings the opening aria: "Perche me, Signore?" (Why me, Lord?)

He sings of the pleasures he has known in this plush assignment.. of battles won and golf balls lost..

Tutto bene..

Enter, stage right, his loyal assistant, Private Party, who sings the refrain "Non Tutto é Perduto, mio Duce." (All is not lost, my leader.)

PHIL, THE ITALIAN SCALLION) Frank

"PRESIDIO" The Dance of the Dying Military Base. Scene II General Quarters, the hero, finds himself caught in a cost-cutting battle with Federal forces.

2-10-89

With his faithful companion he sings "O Del Mio Dolce Ardor" (O Thou Beloved) which tells of his family, the City he loves and the need for a military presence in San Francisco.

Cerco te.. *chiamo te..*

The cost-cutters are saddened by the hero's plea. They weep, succumbing to a deep inner brooding over their roles..

PHIL/MY CUT RUNNETH OVER) Frank

They sing "Stiamo Solo Facendo il Nostro Lavoro" (We are only doing our jobs!) and stab him anyway.

Stiamo Solo.

The Federal cost-cutters, having done their damage, leave, stage right, singing "Da che Parte per Fort Dix?" (Which way to Fort Dix?)

Hope for the dying military presence enters in the form of two liberal representatives (Barbara Boxer, Nancy Pelosi) in the roles of the fairy princesses.

As the general stares in disbelief, the Democratic handmaidens, elected as military watchdogs, do the "Dance of the Rationalized Agenda" in which they plead for the military presence and its local payroll to be saved.

This dance is seldom performed, especially in Birkenstocks.

(FEETS... DO YOUR STUFF) Frank

"PRESIDIO"
The Dance of the Dying Military Base
·Scene IV·
The hero, General Quarters, lies mortally wounded by Federal cost-cutters.

1-12-89

Local park officials, sensing the pending passing of the old general, enter bearing plans for bike paths and hiking trails.

A chorus of developers standing in the wings witness this potential loss of prime real estate.

GASP!

AGUA! AGUA!

They weep openly and sing the timeless lament: "Dove é il Segretareo Watt Quando hai Veramenté Bisogno di lui" (Where is Secretary Watt When you Really Need him?).

©Paul (THE MINUS TOUCH) Frank

"PRESIDIO"
The Dance of the Dying Military Base
·Final Scene·
The hero, General Quarters, succumbs to the wounds inflicted by Federal cost-cutters.

CIAO!

The entire cast, including the liberal handmaidens, the GGNRA park officials, the Mayor and local developers mourn the passing of this great military presence..

... for about two minutes.

Then, to the strains of Wagner's "Cry of the Valkyrie" the largest battle scene ever enacted on stage begins.

IT'S MINE!

NO! IT'S MINE!

MINE! MINE!!

©Paul (PHLEGM AT ELEVEN) Frank

1-13-89

NOW HEAR THIS!! NOW HEAR THIS!! WE'RE ALL UNDER ARREST!

The Coast Guard is ordered to enforce a new **DEA** ruling called "Zero Tolerance," requiring the Coast Guard to seize boats with **any** sign of illegal drugs aboard... even a few marijuana seeds. So I created a new program entitled **"Zero Intelligence"**. It was reprinted in many boating newsletters. Within a month the initial program had quietly sunk.

THE COAST GUARD CUTTER "**STICKLER**" SPEEDS ACROSS SAN FRANCISCO BAY:

What is your mission for today, Captain?

COAST GUARD 211

5-31-88

To follow the guidelines of the U.S. Customs Service's recent "**Zero Intelligence**" drug policy..

I see..

Simply put... "**Act First. Think Later!**"

"Act... First..."

I think I have that written down in Latin in my cabin. I'll be right back.

© Phil (A LATIN LUBBER) Frank

THE '**ZERO INTELLIGENCE**' DRUG POLICY ENFORCEMENT:

Our orders are to seize **any** vessel carrying **any** amount of suspected drugs..

Like this?

6-1-88

WHERE'D YOU GET THIS?

Off the floor... by your foot.

SOUND GENERAL QUARTERS!! **SEIZE THIS SHIP!!**

'AA-OOO-GA! AA-OOO-GA!

© Phil (BEYOND THE 12-MILE REEFER) Frank

Now hear this!! We're all under arrest!

One false move and I get it!

Panel 1: THE CAPTAIN OF THE COAST GUARD CUTTER "**STICKLER**", UPON FINDING SUSPECTED DRUGS ABOARD, ORDERS THE BOAT SEIZED.

Now what, Sir?

We're taking ourselves in tow..

Panel 2: *Excuse me, cap'n.. ..but has anyone seen a bag of oregano from the galley?*

Panel 3: *Hey! Dat's it! Tanks a lot!*

© Phil (YOU DID SAY SEIZE 'ER SALAD...) Frank

Panel 4: *Well...ahem!...That solves that! I trust none of this will appear in print..*

Oh, you have my word on it, sir..

6-2-88

Since I'm taking aim at waterborne government agencies I think I'll shoot at another – B.C.D.C. (Bay Conservation & Development Commission). This agency was attacking the anchored-out houseboats off Sausalito and particularly a boat named "Forbes' Island" and its builder/owner Forbes Kidoo. Being from Sausalito and a 13 year resident of an 1890's houseboat, I was biased on Forbes' side. Does it show?

Panel 1: MANY A TALL SHIP HAS PLIED THE WATERS OF SAN FRANCISCO BAY, BUT NONE SO FORMIDABLE AS THIS..

C.REEAK

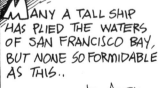

Panel 2: THE FIRST MATE OF THIS FLAGSHIP OF THE **BAY CONSERVATION AND DEVELOPMENT COMMISSION** ADDRESSES THE CAPTAIN:

Orders of the day, Sir?

10-27-87

Panel 3: BCDC CAPTAIN HORATIO BAYFILL BARKS HIS ORDERS..

Steer for Sausalito and prepare for a legal assault on the houseboat known as "Forbes Island".

ALL LAWYERS ON DECK!!

© Phil (A STERN..WARNING) Frank

Panel 4: *♪ YO..HO..HO... ..AND A ROLL O' RED TAPE!!*

PRIDE OF BUREAUCRACY

WIDE IN THE STERN AND HEAVY IN THE BILGE, THE "PRIDE OF BUREAUCRACY" ENTERS THE WATERS OFF SAUSALITO..

BLIGHT HO!!

BCDC CAPTAIN HORATIO BAYFILL PEERS THROUGH HIS SPYGLASS:

ARGH! There's the canker now.. Forbes Island ... as scurrilous a sight of illegal flotsam as has ever crossed my bow..

10-26-87

Gee... Captain I think it's rather nice...

Thinking can get you into trouble on this ship, mate!!

© Phil (LIVE FREE OR DIVE!) Frank

BCDC'S FLAGSHIP, THE "PRIDE OF BUREAUCRACY" HOVES TO NEAR ITS TARGET.. "FORBES' ISLAND," A HOUSEBOAT OFF SAUSALITO.

Steady as you go, Mister Yesman.

Yes, Sir..

PREPARE TO FIRE A LEGAL BROADSIDE..

AYE, AYE, SIR.

10-27-87

"By order of his majesty myself, I declare Forbes Island illegal, creative, fun-loving and therefore unfit to exist."

FIRE WHEN READY!!

FIRING IN TRIPLICATE SIR!!

BOOM! BOOM! BOOM!

That'll teach 'im!

© Phil (SHORT JOHN SILVER) Frank

Hummm, Baby!!

Giants Fever... Hum Baby!... Giant Attitude. They win, they lose... they slump... they soar.. they need a new home. They're our team and their fans are loyal through it all. And who could be more loyal than a bear named Alphonse?

GIANTS

ALPHONSE AWAKENS TO THE SUDDEN REALIZATION THAT THE **GIANTS** MAY HAVE WON THEIR DIVISION BUT **NOT** THE PENNANT..

GULP!

..NOT UNTIL THEY BEAT CHICAGO.

BEAT THE CUBS!! BEAT THE CUBS!!

SCREE!!

BEEP!!

BEAT THOSE CUBS!

CLUB THOSE STUPID BEARS!

CLUB THOSE..

Doc, does this mean I'm masochistic?

Vell, at least they're not the Chicago Harp Seals..

BEAT THE CUBS!

The day this strip ran, the Giants put the same message on their screen during the Houston game.

IT'S LATE JULY.. A BEAUTIFUL SUMMER DAY AND AN AFTERNOON GAME AT **CANDLESTICK**..

Not just **anyone** gets to share my reserved seats, Franklin..

I'm honored..

All I've got to say, Alphonse.. is you are one heck of a Giants fan and I hope they..

Oooh! Oooh!

HOUSTON GIANTS

THE GIANTS WELCOME **ALPHONSE** OF THE **FOG CITY DUMPSTER**

Excuse me while I relish my fifteen seconds of fame..

Speaking of relish..

IT'S A QUIET MONDAY MORNING IN THE VAST EMPTINESS OF CANDLESTICK PARK:

Why do I let you talk me into these things? We could be arrested for sneaking in here!

Shh, Hilda! This is a very solemn moment.

AT SECOND BASE, ALPHONSE PERFORMS A RITUAL, DICTATED BY HIS BIOLOGICAL CLOCK, MARKING THE END OF THE REGULAR BASEBALL SEASON.

THE INCENSE AND FOOD ARE ENTICEMENTS TO THE GODS SO THAT IN SPRING THE PLAYERS WILL AGAIN RETURN TO THE VERDANT INFIELD.

HUMMMMMMMMM BABY!!

You're making an offering of Polish dogs and nachos?

Trust me, Hilda. It's worked every year so far.

It's as we feared.. "World Series Fever."

NNNNNNNN.

The Bay Area was hardly thinking about earthquakes in the early weeks of October 1989. They had a cross-bay World Series on their hands.. The Giants would play the Oakland A's. This caused problems for fans who'd rooted for both teams over the years.

OUR URBANIZED BEAR FACES A CONFUSING FUTURE. CLAD IN A **GIANTS** T-SHIRT AND AN OAKLAND **A's** HAT, HE CLUTCHES A SAN FRANCISCO BANNER IN ONE PAW AND AN **ATHLETICS** SEAT CUSHION IN THE OTHER..

10-12-89

THIS IS A BRUIN IN A SERIOUS QUANDARY. WHERE DO HIS TRUE LOYALTIES LIE? FOR WHOM DOES HE ROOT?

Life is **SO** complicated..

Sometimes I miss the good old days in the woods when the only decision was what to rip open first... the cooler or the knapsack..

©Phil (THE WURST IS YET TO COME) Frank

You bozo! Root for the A's! They'll sweep the series!

Don't listen to him, Alphonse! You're a Giants fan!

10-13-89

You rooted for them for years!.. ...Even when they were out of the running !!

STICK IT IN YOUR HALO, GOODY TWO PAWS!!

Listen, Alphonse.. Stick with the A's. Even the hot dogs are better at the Coliseum!

To tempt the soul with the desires of the flesh is the work of the devil!!

SO WHAT? I **AM** THE DEVIL!

OHHHH.

©Phil (HABEAS CORRUPTUS) Frank

GIANTS FEVER SWEEPS CITY! TYPICALLY NORMAL INDIVIDUALS PERFORM STRANGE ACTS:

Heddo... dis is Mayor Art Agnew calling... I wunt 4 Series tickets sent to P.O. Box 2591 Brisbane..

10-16-89

FASHION MAVENS FACE THE ULTIMATE TEST:

DOES BLACK AND ORANGE LOOK BETTER WITH CHECKS OR STRIPES?

All **I** have to do is put on an orange tie..

AND FANS FLIP OUT..

MURRAY THE FURRIER

I'd like my right side dyed orange and my left side black..

AS THE WORLD SERIES COMES TO SAN FRANCISCO FOR THE FIRST TIME IN 27 YEARS...

They're baaaack.

©PAUL (THEY CAME FROM BEYOND THE BRIDGE) FRANK

Ohhhhhhhh.. ♪ **Take** me out to the ball game ♪

CANDLE

SO GET IN ALREADY!!

Take me out to the crowd... ♪♪

Hey! turn it down, dude!

10-17-89

Buy me some peanuts and Cracker Jacks.. ♪♪

No Cracker Jack: How about nachos?

I don't care if I **never** come back!! ♪

Throw the key away..

STADIUM SECURITY

©PAUL (LET MY PEOPLE GO!) FRANK

Oh, it's Root, Root Root for the home team... ♪♪

CANSECO IS GOING BACK, BACK.... HE TRIPS OVER A FERAL PIG!!

10-18-89

If they don't win it's a shame.... ♪♪

for it's.. ♪ ♪ ♪ ..ONE.. TWO.. THREE STRIKES YOU'RE OUT!!

WHAP! WHAP! WHAP!

©PAUL (THE BEAR FAX) FRANK

At the old ball game!!

GIANTS

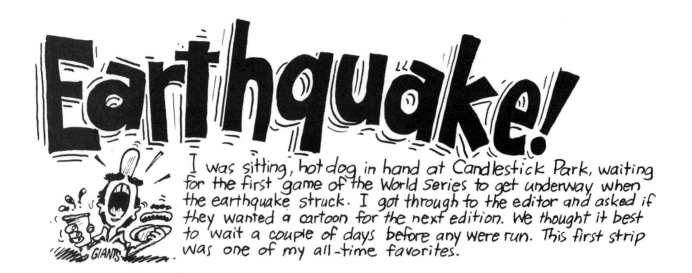

Earthquake!

I was sitting, hot dog in hand at Candlestick Park, waiting for the first game of the World Series to get underway when the earthquake struck. I got through to the editor and asked if they wanted a cartoon for the next edition. We thought it best to wait a couple of days before any were run. This first strip was one of my all-time favorites.

TWO QUAKE SURVIVORS TALK ABOUT THE EXPERIENCE:

Where were you when it hit, Alphonse?

I was at the baseball game, Olive.

10-20-89

I was home all alone and the whole house was shaking. I did everything I was supposed to do in case of an earthquake. I was _real_ brave.

But you know what?

What?

I was real scared too.

Well, you know what..

Big bears get scared too!

© Phil (Gimme a bear hug!) Frank

Hmm..

10-21-89

Hmm..

What do you think?

Well.. it's relatively stable but this is an old panel design. It has no reinforcement.

© Phil (Drawn and Quartered) Frank

Will it have to come down?

Let's wait until the engineer from the Federal Comics Commission gets here.

Strip 1 (10-23-89):

ENGINEERS FROM THE **FCC** (FEDERAL COMICS COMMISSION) DO A SEISMIC STABILITY CHECK OF THE STRIP.

These are awfully thin walls for a San Francisco cartoon.

You're right about that, Chief.

Is the owner here?

Right here.

He's right here, chief.

I want all these panels reinforced. Thicker lines! Notice the buckling in this panel?

Yes. I see that.

Does anyone else occupy this space?

Well... some bears, a raven, a metermaid, her daughter Olive, some feral pigs, a guru, an undercover agent named Tuslō and a cable car gripman..

Only in San Francisco..

©Phil (ALL IN THE FAMILY) Frank

Strip 2 (10-24-89):

THE HEAD OF THE **FEDERAL COMICS COMMISSION** FROM WASHINGTON D.C. SURVEYS THE STABILITY OF THE STRIP.

I don't like these thin walls. Make a note of that!

Yes, sir.

What's above this space?

I'm not sure, sir... ..but there's a hatch.

Holy Toledo!! There must be ten tons of type up there!!

Pretty scary.

Where are you going, Chief?

Uh.. I think an **external** survey is definitely in order!

Phil (ON THE OUTSIDE LOOKING IN) Frank

Strip 3 (10-24-89):

THE CORPORATE HEADQUARTERS OF **"ONE-HOUR ENLIGHTENMENT"** LIE IN RUINS.. CHIEF EXECUTIVE OFFICER **BABA RE BOK** STUDIES THE SCENE AND PHILOSOPHIZES..

My computer.. my FAX.. my mailing lists..

FAX BABA 332-9197

What lie here are but material goods, crutches of a capitalistic society..

To lose these is to lose nothing.. ..as long as one does not lose his spirit and love of life..

I couldn't agree more!

My insurance agent, no doubt..

©Phil (SIGN ON THE DOTTED LION) Frank

"Residents of many Marina district dwellings are being allowed only 15 minutes to gather personal belongings before buildings are to be torn down..."

Fifteen minutes? How could a person possibly decide what possessions to take in only fifteen minutes?

Hmm...

Tick Tick Tick

?

Four National Geographics, a cactus, one tennis shoe, your Lincoln penny collection, your Giants cap, the jigsaw puzzle with two pieces missing and your passport.

Let me guess. You're going to Tibet to have a garage sale?

Tick Tick Tick

ORCHIDS.. TO ART AGNOS FOR HIS LEADERSHIP DURING THE EARTHQUAKE CRISIS..

Pour moi?

ONIONS... TO THE NETWORK NEWS ANCHORS IN THEIR STRETCH LIMOUSINES..

No thanks.. ..We have fresh fruit..

ORCHIDS.. TO THE THOUSANDS OF VOLUNTEERS WHOSE EFFORTS HAVE HELPED SO MANY..

ONIONS TO THE FEW STORES THAT PRICE-GOUGED PEOPLE ON BATTERIES, WATER, AND FOOD IMMEDIATELY AFTER THE QUAKE..

GROCE

For free? Sure, I'll take it!

OKRA TO THE MILITARY VOLUNTEERS CLEARING DEBRIS WHO WERE PREPARING TO HAUL AWAY THE VAILLANCOURT FOUNTAIN.

What a mess.

Baba.. I've come to grips with the earthquake and all the resulting losses..

Good.

..And I could deal with the rains that followed. ..But when the mudslides began and the funnel clouds touched down..

Yes?

Well... I **know** Mother Nature is trying to tell us something but I don't know what!

That it's okay to live in her house but don't wipe your feet on her carpet!

KNOCK! KNOCK!—

Come in..

We're with the funding wing of the National Endowment for the Arts.. we have information you're an occasional painter.

CLICK!

Well.. yes.. I..find it relaxing..

I see.. what is this you're doing?

(LIFE IS A CABERNET) Frank

It's a still life. I call it "Soggy Cheerios and Cheap Wine".

Cheap wine.. Did you get that..

Got it.

You understand it's nothing personal.. we at the NEA must be very careful these days..

7-19-90

We can't be funding any art that's obscene, unpatriotic or demeaning to the social fiber of the nation..

He subscribes to "Mother Jones".

CLICK!

It's our job to assess the cultural acceptance of each artist's work and lifestyle.

Check out his refrigerator!

CLICK!

(I HAVE AN ICE DAY) Frank

Well, I haven't even **applied** for an NEA grant.

Well, our advice is.. ..DON'T!

CLICK!

Dear Mr. Farley,
The National Endowment for the Arts has funded many aspiring artists in the past.

Two of our evaluators recently visited your studio to review your work-in-progress.. "Soggy Cheerios with Red Wine"

We find your work to be derivative, trite, pedantic and naive with virtually no artistic merit. You offer little challenge to the established powers in government, business and education.

7-22-90

(BENNIES FROM HEAVEN) Frank

Enclosed is a check for $2500. Congratulations.

The "Summer of Love"... San Francisco, 1967. It's twenty years later and, in a fit of nostalgia for the recent past, residents drag out their peace symbols, love beads and Fillmore posters and head down to Haight and Ashbury to "dig it"... ...the time capsule, that is.

AN AGING GURU DIGS INTO HIS CHEST OF MEMORIES:

Yessir.. the Sixties.. I remember the way it REALLY was..

..Our beautiful youth blindly trusting everyone!!

Naively seeking spiritual truth from opportunistic charlatans..

Giving away their inheritances to finance pie-in-the-sky communes run by narcissistic leaders.

Ahh... those were the days..

©Phil (I'M INCENSED!) Frank

You should be honored, Baba.. ..being chosen to dig up the time capsule buried at Haight and Ashbury..

Indeed I am... ..but I've got to dress for the occasion.

Here's my old tie-dyed robe.. ..and my love beads!!

And here's my peace symbol!... ..and my sandals!

What do you know!! I can still fit into my old uniform!

©Phil (TRANQS FOR THE MEMORIES) Frank

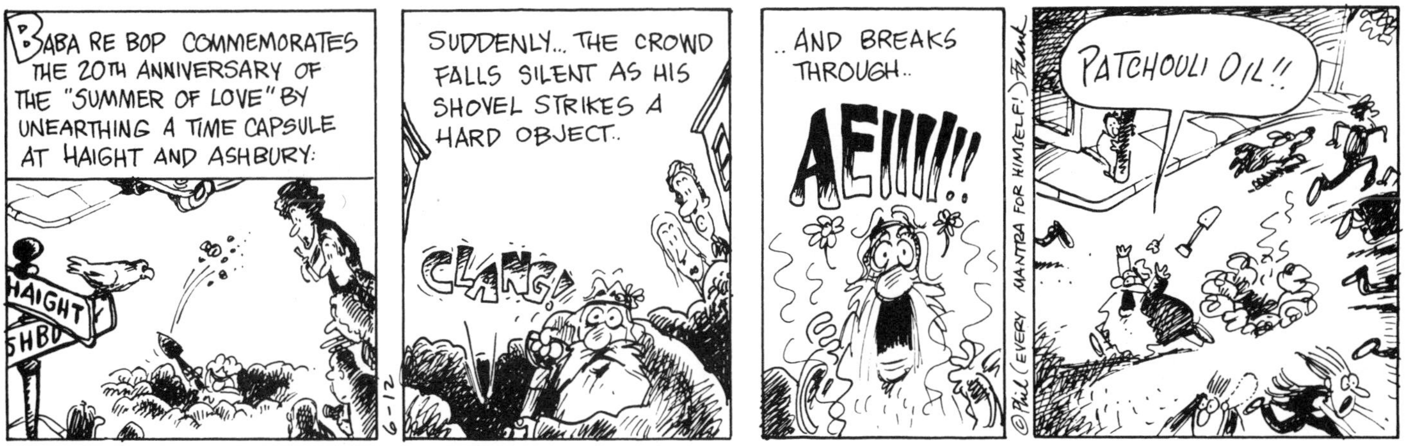
BABA RE BOP COMMEMORATES THE 20TH ANNIVERSARY OF THE "SUMMER OF LOVE" BY UNEARTHING A TIME CAPSULE AT HAIGHT AND ASHBURY:
HAIGHT
SHBU
6-12
SUDDENLY... THE CROWD FALLS SILENT AS HIS SHOVEL STRIKES A HARD OBJECT..
CLANG!
..AND BREAKS THROUGH..
AEIIII!!
PATCHOULI OIL!!
© Phil (EVERY MANTRA FOR HIMSELF!) Frank

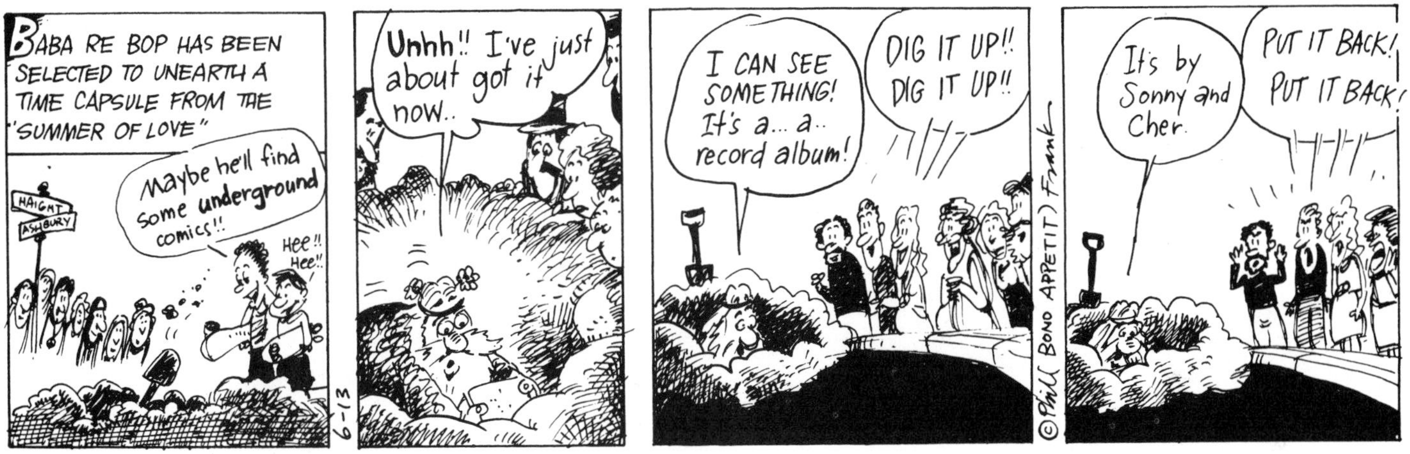
BABA RE BOP HAS BEEN SELECTED TO UNEARTH A TIME CAPSULE FROM THE "SUMMER OF LOVE"
HAIGHT
ASHBURY
Maybe he'll find some **underground** comics!!
Hee!! Hee!!
6-13
Unhh!! I've just about got it now..
I CAN SEE SOMETHING! It's a... a.. record album!
DIG IT UP!! DIG IT UP!!
© Phil (BONO APPETIT) Frank
It's by Sonny and Cher.
PUT IT BACK! PUT IT BACK!

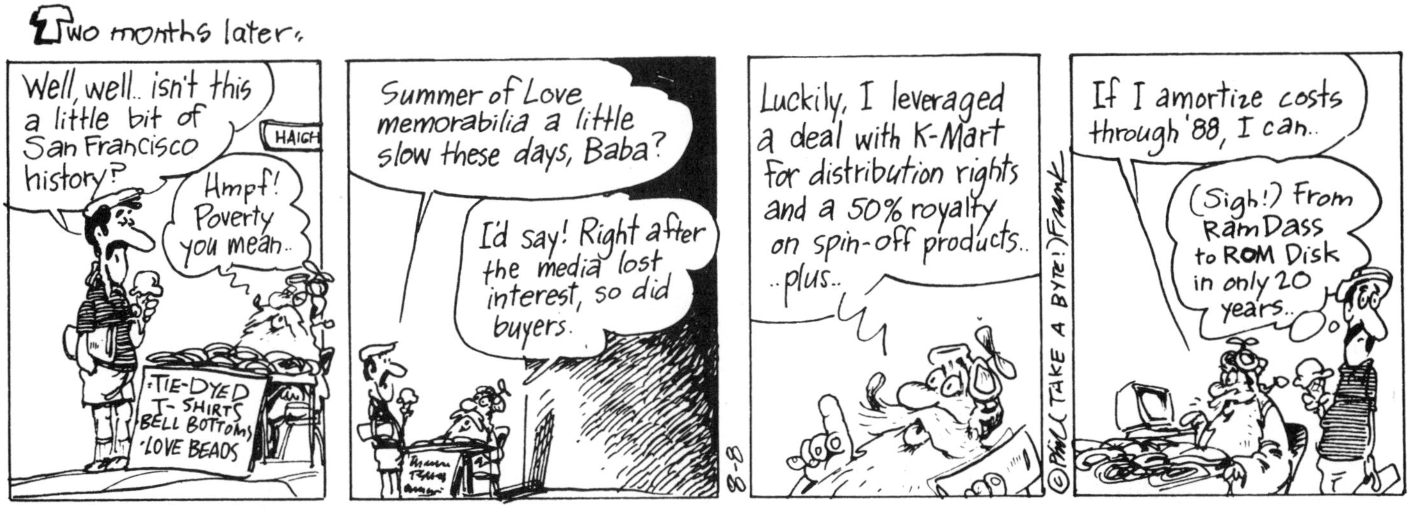
Two months later..
Well, well.. isn't this a little bit of San Francisco history?
HAIGH
Hmpf! Poverty you mean..
TIE-DYED T-SHIRTS BELL BOTTOMS LOVE BEADS
Summer of Love memorabilia a little slow these days, Baba?
I'd say! Right after the media lost interest, so did buyers.
8-8
Luckily, I leveraged a deal with K-Mart for distribution rights and a 50% royalty on spin-off products.. ..plus..
© Phil (TAKE A BYTE!) Frank
If I amortize costs through '88, I can..
(Sigh!) From Ram Dass to **ROM** Disk in only 20 years..

As the fitness craze sweeps through San Francisco, almost everyone gets caught up in the calorie-counting, deep-squatting, Spandex-stretching experience...

...even a 450 pound California black bear named Bruin Hilda.

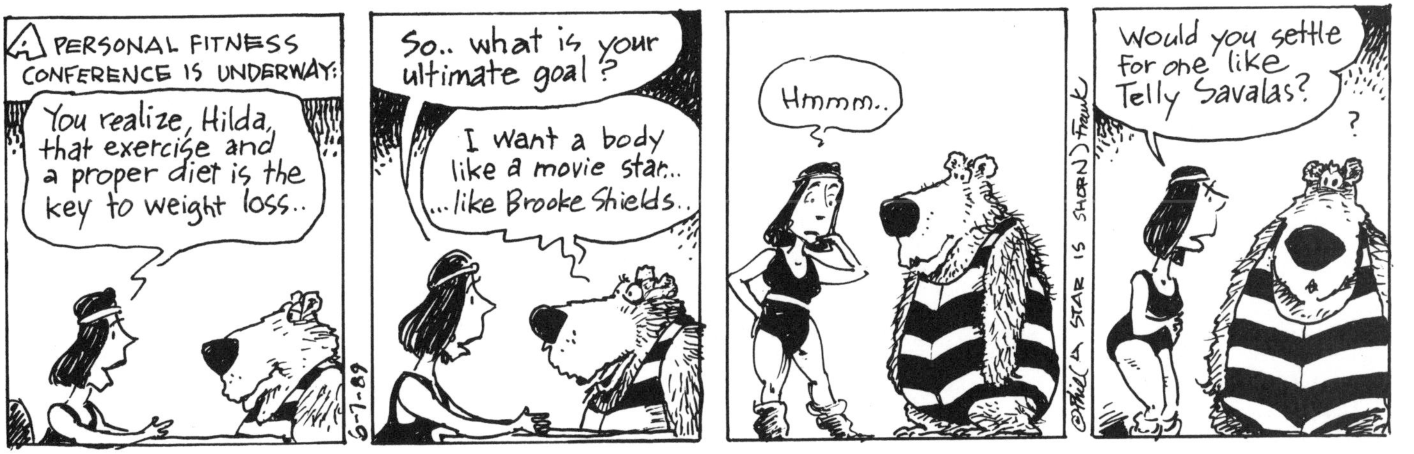
A PERSONAL FITNESS CONFERENCE IS UNDERWAY:
You realize, Hilda, that exercise and a proper diet is the key to weight loss..
6-7-89
So.. what is your ultimate goal?
I want a body like a movie star.. ...like Brooke Shields..
Hmmm..
©Phil (A STAR IS SHORN) Frank
Would you settle for one like Telly Savalas?
?

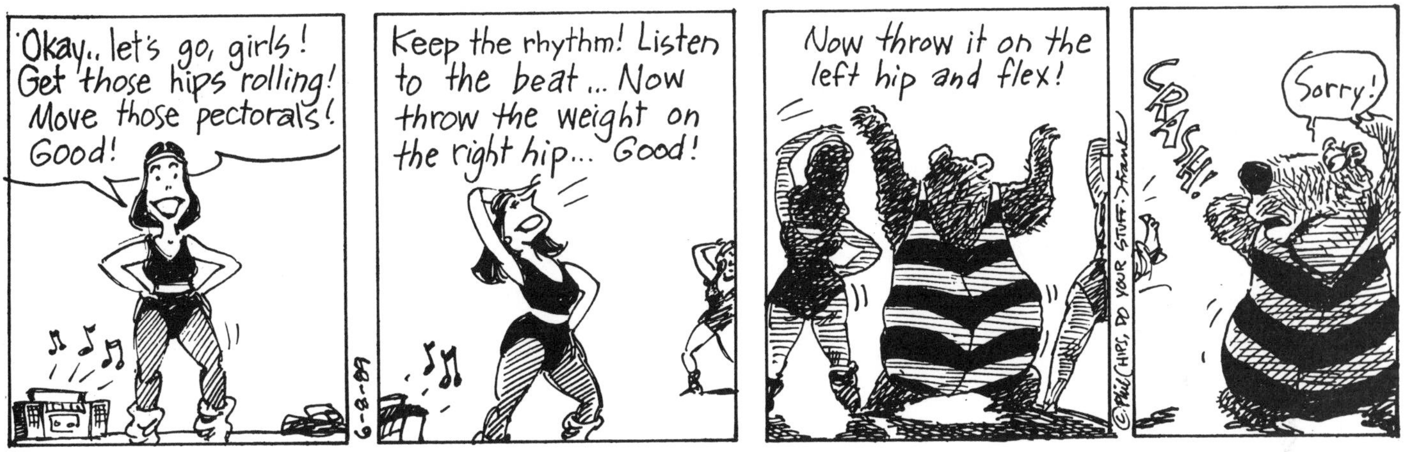
Okay.. let's go, girls! Get those hips rolling! Move those pectorals! Good!
6-8-89
Keep the rhythm! Listen to the beat ... Now throw the weight on the right hip... Good!
Now throw it on the left hip and flex!
©Phil (HIPS, DO YOUR STUFF.) Frank
CRASH!
Sorry!

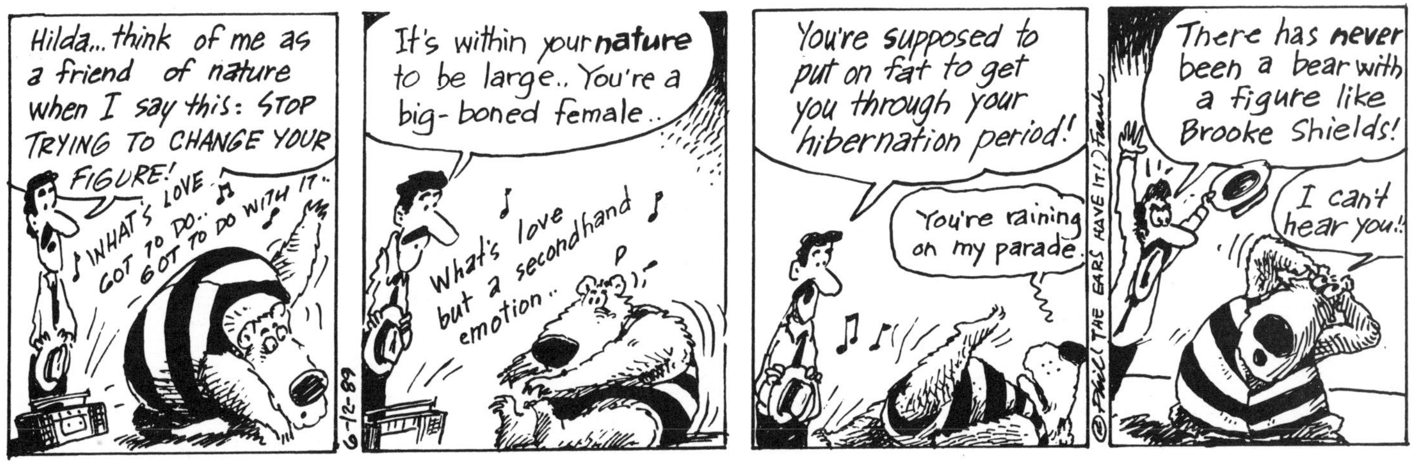
Hilda... think of me as a friend of nature when I say this: STOP TRYING TO CHANGE YOUR FIGURE!
WHAT'S LOVE GOT TO DO.. GOT TO DO WITH IT..
6-12-89
It's within your **nature** to be large.. You're a big-boned female..
What's love but a secondhand emotion..
You're supposed to put on fat to get you through your hibernation period!
You're raining on my parade..
©Phil (THE EARS HAVE IT!) Frank
There has **never** been a bear with a figure like Brooke Shields!
I can't hear you!!

It is not unusual for mail to arrive at the Chronicle addressed to "Farley". One such letter arrived shortly after the kidnapping of the UC Berkeley mascot, a stuffed Grizzly bear. A typed note indicated that the bear was in good hands and would eventually be released. Enclosed with the note was a Polaroid photo of the bear clad in a Stanford t-shirt. We set up a "hot-line" at the paper. All the calls were about stuffed teddy bears seen in parked cars. A few months later the bear was released unharmed.

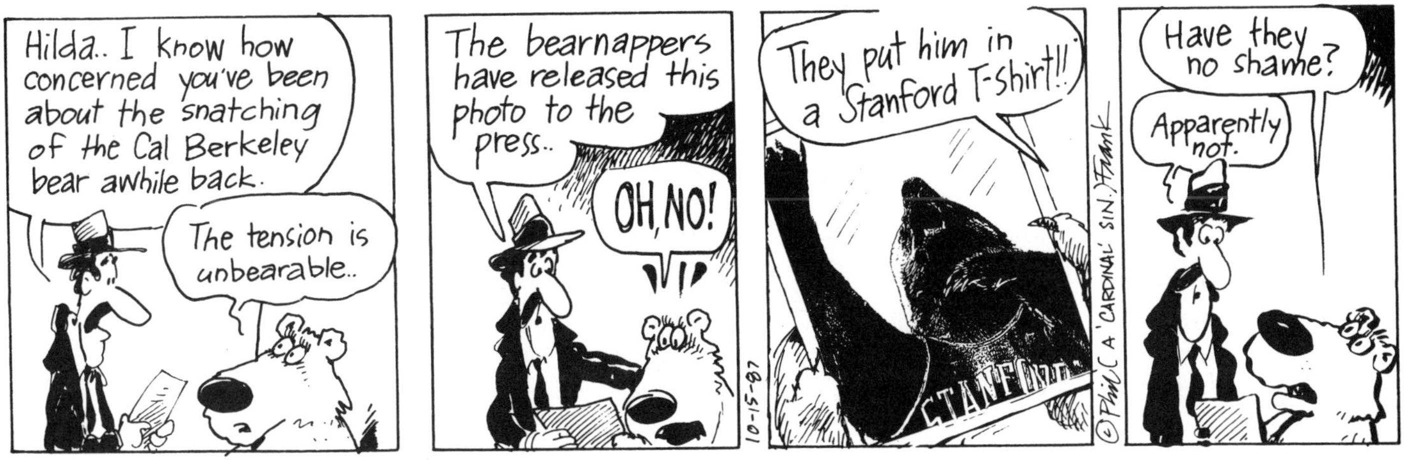
Hilda.. I know how concerned you've been about the snatching of the Cal Berkeley bear awhile back.
The tension is unbearable..
The bearnappers have released this photo to the press..
OH, NO!
10-15-87
They put him in a Stanford T-shirt!!
STANFORD
© Phil ('A 'CARDINAL' SIN.) Frank
Have they no shame?
Apparently not.

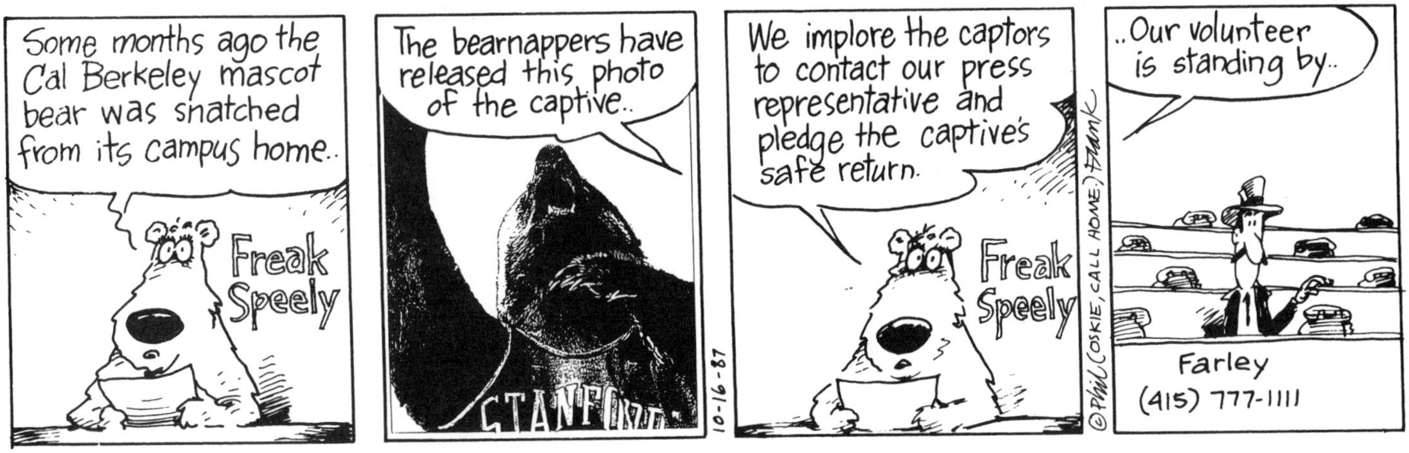
Some months ago the Cal Berkeley mascot bear was snatched from its campus home..
Freak Speely
The bearnappers have released this photo of the captive..
STANFORD
10-16-87
We implore the captors to contact our press representative and pledge the captive's safe return.
Freak Speely
© Phil (OSKIE, CALL HOME.) Frank
..Our volunteer is standing by..
Farley
(415) 777-1111

This strip ran the morning after the bear was released.

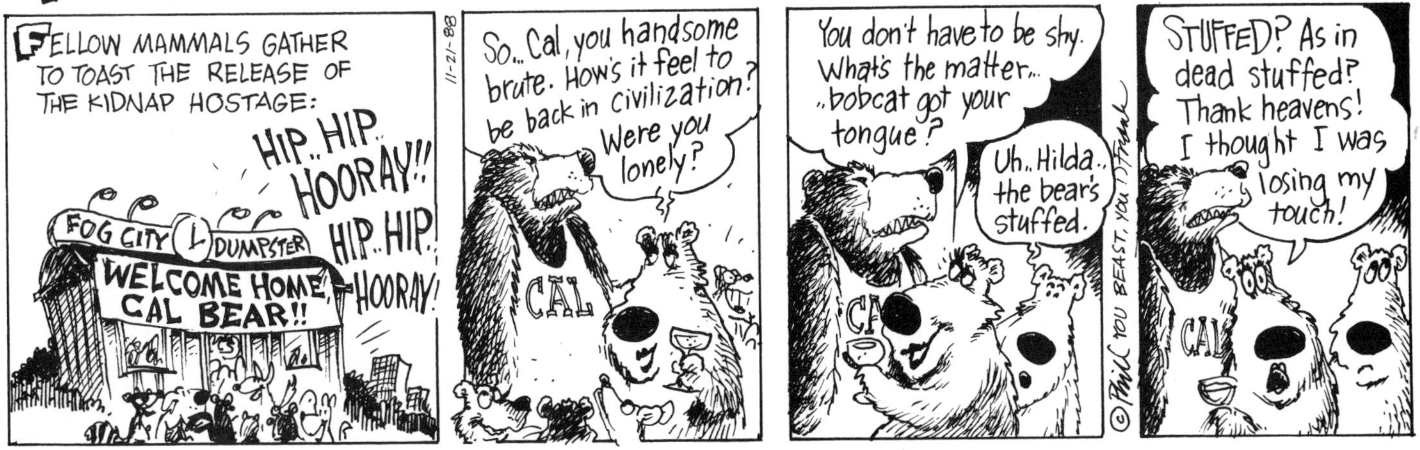
FELLOW MAMMALS GATHER TO TOAST THE RELEASE OF THE KIDNAP HOSTAGE:
HIP.. HIP.. HOORAY!!
HIP.. HIP.. HOORAY!
FOG CITY DUMPSTER
WELCOME HOME CAL BEAR!!
11-21-88
So... Cal, you handsome brute. How's it feel to be back in civilization?
Were you lonely?
CAL
You don't have to be shy. What's the matter... ..bobcat got your tongue?
Uh.. Hilda.. the bear's stuffed.
© Phil (YOU BEAST, YOU!) Frank
STUFFED? As in dead stuffed? Thank heavens! I thought I was losing my touch!

The S&L debacle was just getting up to speed so I sent **Farley** off to get an auto loan from First Feral Savings and Loan. The day the first strip of the series ran I received a phone call from the president of the very solvent First **Federal** Savings and Loan. We had a friendly chat about the series. I thought it wise to change the name of the pigs' firm. Coincidently, First Federal holds the note on our house!

What do you want?

I want to see about getting an auto loan..

Sorry. We close at three..

Three? The sign says nine to five!

Those aren't our hours. Those are the odds of whether or not we keep this place afloat!

Oh..

Hey, listen... we're in the **business** of making risky loans.. That's what made America great!!

Pigs-R-Us
Savings and Loan

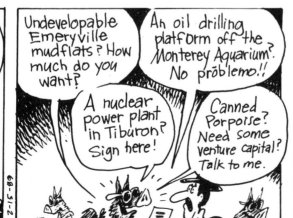

Undevelopable Emeryville mudflats? How much do you want?

A nuclear power plant in Tiburon? Sign here!

An oil drilling platform off the Monterey Aquarium? No problemo!!

Canned Porpoise? Need some venture capital? Talk to me.

PORK BELLY FUTURES?

Now just a minute! **That's** going to cost a little more!

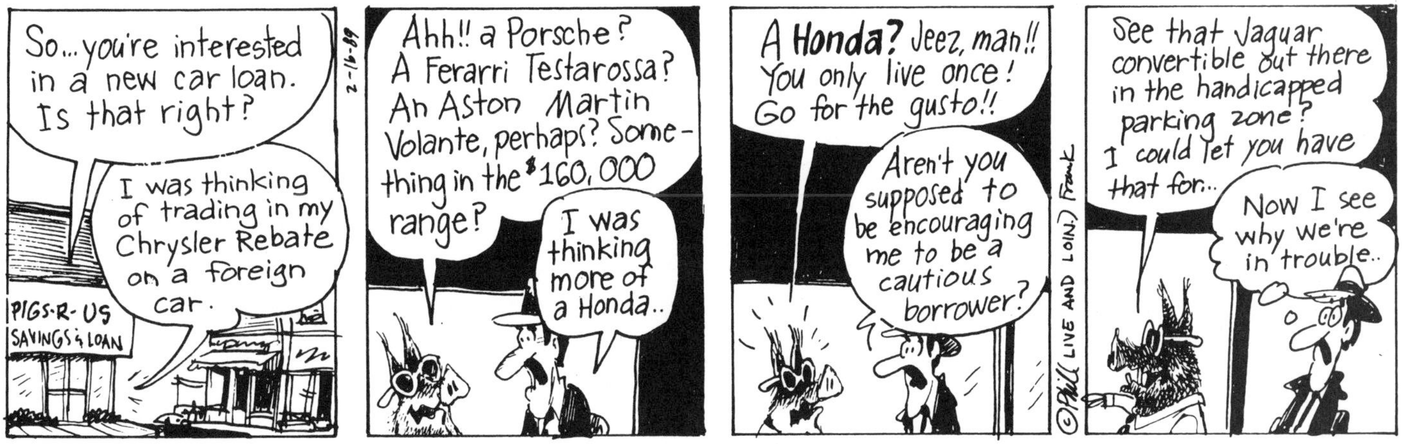
So... you're interested in a new car loan. Is that right?
I was thinking of trading in my Chrysler Rebate on a foreign car.
PIGS-R-US SAVINGS & LOAN
2-16-89
Ahh!! a Porsche? A Ferarri Testarossa? An Aston Martin Volante, perhaps? Something in the $160,000 range?
I was thinking more of a Honda..
A Honda? Jeez, man!! You only live once! Go for the gusto!!
Aren't you supposed to be encouraging me to be a cautious borrower?
©Phil (LIVE AND LOIN.) Frank
See that Jaguar convertible out there in the handicapped parking zone? I could let you have that for...
Now I see why we're in trouble..

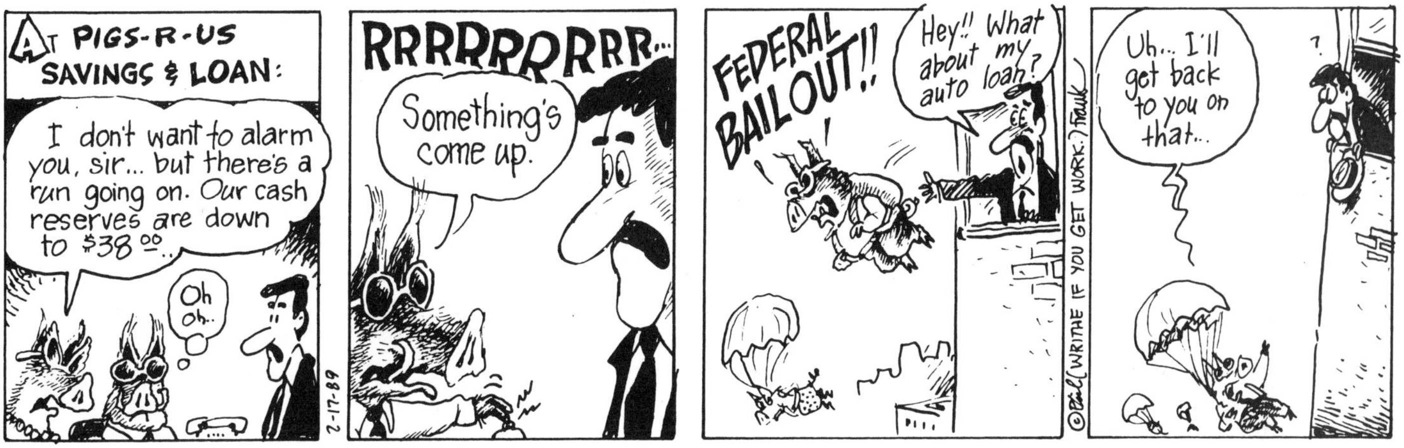
AT PIGS-R-US SAVINGS & LOAN:
I don't want to alarm you, sir... but there's a run going on. Our cash reserves are down to $38.00...
Oh oh..
2-17-89
RRRRRRRRR...
Something's come up.
FEDERAL BAILOUT!!
Hey!! What about my auto loan?
©Phil (WRITHE IF YOU GET WORK.) Frank
Uh... I'll get back to you on that...

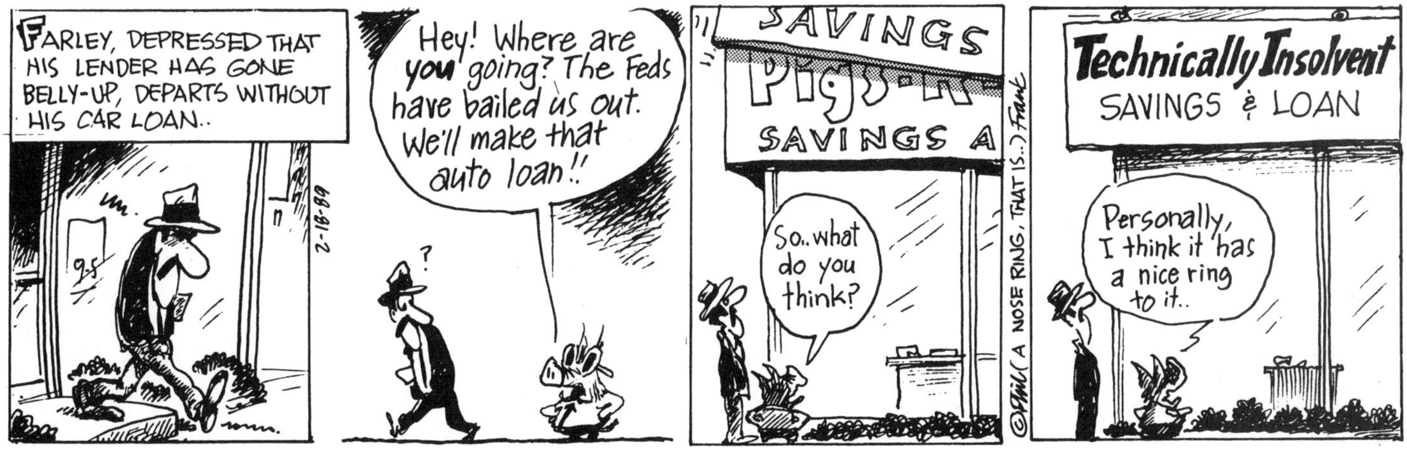
FARLEY, DEPRESSED THAT HIS LENDER HAS GONE BELLY-UP, DEPARTS WITHOUT HIS CAR LOAN..
2-18-89
Hey! Where are you going? The Feds have bailed us out. We'll make that auto loan!!
SAVINGS
SAVINGS A
So.. what do you think?
©Phil (A NOSE RING, THAT IS..) Frank
Technically Insolvent
SAVINGS & LOAN
Personally, I think it has a nice ring to it..

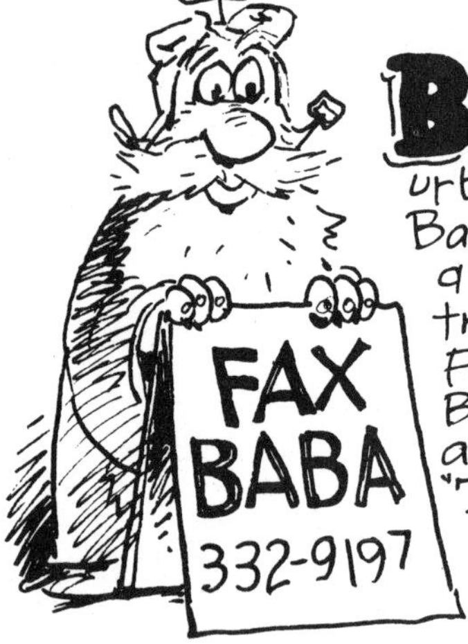
FAX
BABA
332-9197

Baba gets a FAX! Trying to reach out to the young urban professional and maybe get some free tennies, Baba Re Bop changes his last name to ReBok and offers a 1 hour enlightenment course for the time-pressed truth seeker. The FAX number is real and many of the FAXes have worked their way into the strip. When Baba asked for help with the decision over Farley and Irene's relationship, 400 FAXes poured in. "This World" ran a two-page spread of the best.

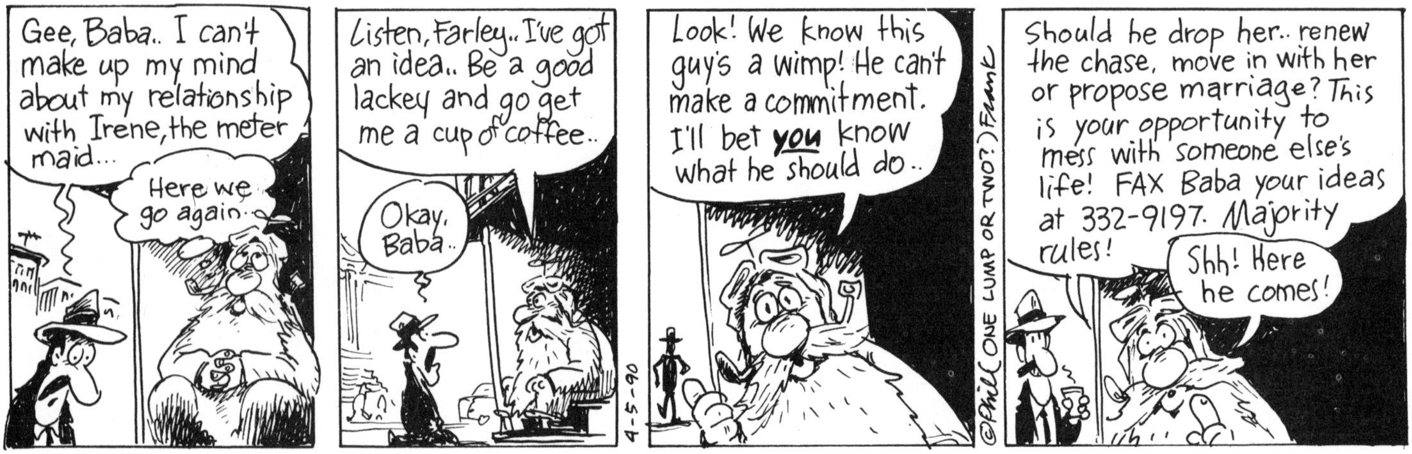
Gee, Baba.. I can't make up my mind about my relationship with Irene, the meter maid...
Here we go again..
Listen, Farley.. I've got an idea.. Be a good lackey and go get me a cup of coffee..
Okay, Baba..
4-5-90
Look! We know this guy's a wimp! He can't make a commitment. I'll bet **you** know what he should do..
©Phil Frank (ONE LUMP OR TWO?)
Should he drop her.. renew the chase, move in with her or propose marriage? This is your opportunity to mess with someone else's life! FAX Baba your ideas at 332-9197. Majority rules!
Shh! Here he comes!

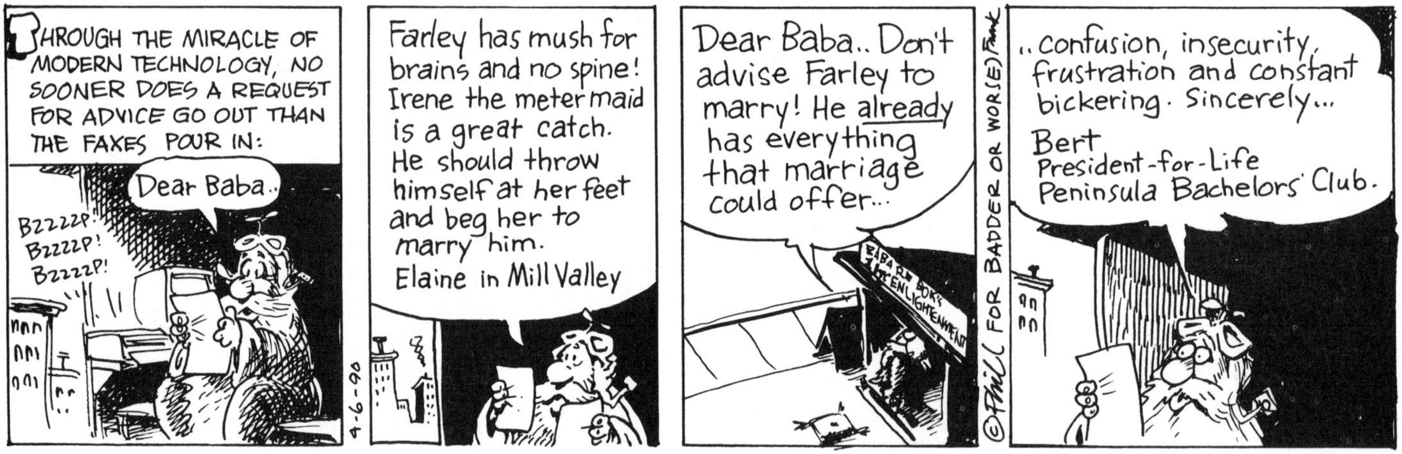
THROUGH THE MIRACLE OF MODERN TECHNOLOGY, NO SOONER DOES A REQUEST FOR ADVICE GO OUT THAN THE FAXES POUR IN:
Dear Baba..
BZZZZP! BZZZZP! BZZZZP!
4-6-90
Farley has mush for brains and no spine! Irene the meter maid is a great catch. He should throw himself at her feet and beg her to marry him.
Elaine in Mill Valley
Dear Baba.. Don't advise Farley to marry! He already has everything that marriage could offer...
©Phil Frank (FOR BADDER OR WORS(E))
..confusion, insecurity, frustration and constant bickering. Sincerely...
Bert
President-for-Life
Peninsula Bachelors' Club.

BABA WATCHES IN TOTAL AMAZEMENT AS HIS **FAX** MACHINE CONTINUES TO POUR OUT READER ADVICE ABOUT **FARLEY'S** LOVE LIFE:

BZZZZZP!
BZZZZZP!!
BZZZZP!!
BZZZZP!.

"Don't be a wimp! Propose marriage!"

"Farley should move in with Irene. But check with her first."

"JUNE WEDDING!"

"Sign a **non**-nuptial agreement and move in!"

"HE SHOULD DUMP HER!"

"She should dump **him**. He's a wimp!"

"RENEW THE CHASE!"

"Make Farley a house-husband!"

"Forget about the relationship! Have them buy a house and make the **real** commitment.. ...a mortgage."

4-9-90

SO MUCH ADVICE IS COMING IN ON **FARLEY'S** LOVE LIFE THAT **BABA** HAS HAD TO LEASE ADJACENT SPACE AND HIRE AN ASSISTANT:

BZZZP!
BZZZP!
BZZZP!

FAX BABA 332-9197

Okay, Beppo.. "MARRY IRENE" in that pile.. "MOVE IN WITH HER" in that pile.. "DROP THE RELATIONSHIP" in that pile..

Okay..

4-10-90

I'll go get some more!

What about Irene dropping **him**?

Make a pile labeled **WIMP!**

What a weird job...

BABA REVIEWS THE FAXES ON FARLEY'S LOVE LIFE:

Dear Baba... I think Farley should move in with Irene. Things could get kinda kinky..

4-11-90

She's such a dominant personality. She could wear her meter maid uniform in the bedroom...

She could smack him with her chalk stick and threaten to give him tickets if he isn't a good boy. It could be fun. A fan.

What have I created?

ORDER BEGINS TO EMERGE FROM THE CHAOS OF FAXES..

The biggest stack recommends that Farley should move in with Irene, Baba..

Okay..

4-12-90

Coming in a strong second is "MARRIAGE OR PROPOSAL THEREOF"

Followed by "RENEW THE CHASE"

Okay..

Hey, Baba.. ..what are you doing?

Not much, Farley... ..just..

Farley?

WHAT'RE YOU DOING HERE? THIS IS A SECRET PROJECT! OUT OF MY BUSINESS!!

©PHIL (ONE MORE TIME, WITH FILLING) FRANK

"Doing our best to shape your future."

OUT!

The strangest thing, Bruce.. I stopped by to talk to Baba yesterday..

Yes?

And he **threw me out!** Said he was working on a secret project..

Oh?

I got the feeling he was up to no good so I said..

4-13-90

©PHIL (CONSUMER RETORTS) FRANK

Listen to **this** FAX— "Farley should renew the chase — this comic strip needs more sex, lies and videotape"

Took the words right out of my beak!!

BEPPO HAS ORGANIZED THE **FAX**ES INTO CATEGORIES:

Okay, Baba.. so far Sixty-two say "MOVE IN WITH IRENE"

Forty-four say "MARRIAGE SHOULD BE PROPOSED"

Okay..

Eight say "FARLEY SHOULD DROP THE RELATIONSHIP."

And then there's this one..

Fifteen say "KEEP THE RELATIONSHIP AS IT IS"

Okay..

4-14-90

"We suspect Farley's confusion may be more deep-rooted. We suggest Farley find out if Irene has an eligible brother."

©PHIL (SURREAL LIFE GUY) FRANK

That's a switch.

Better start a new pile.

BABA REVIEWS THE LAST OF THE FAXES ABOUT **FARLEY**'S LOVE LIFE:

That's it! Whew!!

Have you reached a decision, Most Hairy One?

I have, Beppo... and I will give Farley my decision next week..

4-27-90

His life will be forever changed and we, each of us, will have taken part in altering the course of his life..

(Gulp.)

© Phil (TRANCENDENTAL MEDICATION) Frank

Playing God sure makes me thirsty..

BAR

Farley.. you came to me a month ago seeking guidance in your relationship with Irene..

That's true, Baba.

I have been deep in meditation and have had much input from many.. ..er.. experts..

and?

It's time for a change in your life, Farley...

CHANGE? As in BIG... scare-the-wits-out-of-me-run-away-and-hide change?

© Phil I WORK WITHOUT A NET. Frank

More like...this-is something-I've-never-done-before-in-my-life-but-I'll probably-live-through-it change.

I'm still here...

Okay.. so let's say I ask Irene to move in together... ...**Then** what?

Then there's the matter of location.

Location? Jeez! I'd better take notes.. ...Okay.

You have to decide between you..Do **you** move in with **her**?

5-3-90

Move in with her?

Do she and her daughter move in with you?

She move in..with.. me.

Or get a new place together?

Or.. new place together.

I'd suggest the latter.

© Phil (RUNG AGAIN.) Frank

Ladder. Okay.. what do I do with the ladder?

A MAN-TO-MYNAH CONVERSATION IS UNDER WAY IN NORTH BEACH:

Bruce.. I'd like to share something with you. There may be a change in our living situation soon.

You're pregnant?

Something even **more** radical!.. a potential shared domicile, with Irene and her daughter.

You, the confirmed bachelor, making a commitment?

5-10-90

Baba thinks it would help to resolve the tension in our relationship.

What does **Irene** think about all this?

Oh.. I haven't mentioned it to her yet..

Well.. any guy who'd discuss this sort of thing with his bird first is obviously a rare catch.

©Phil AS THE WORM TURNS) Frank

Olive.. what would you think of the idea of you and your mom and I living together?

Gee.. that could be fun!!

6-2-90

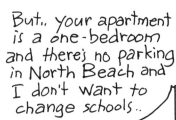

But.. your apartment is a one-bedroom and there's no parking in North Beach and I don't want to change schools..

Well.. there's always **your** house..

True.. but our house only has two bedrooms.. ..mom's and mine.

Where would **you** sleep?

©Phil (RJN FOR THE ROUNDHOUSE :) Frank

Well.. I've cleverly manipulated myself into yet another corner.

Well?

I came as soon as I heard, Farley. Why did Bruce leave?

I'm not sure..

Things were very confusing.. we'd been squabbling a lot about a potential shared domicile..

Shared with whom?

6-28-90

With you and Olive and your cat.. I think it was the cat part that pushed him over the edge..

Me?

I hate to pry.. but was there a reason I wasn't told about your plans?

They were just conceptual ideas... ..There was no plan of attack as yet..

©Phil (PRY HARDER.) Frank

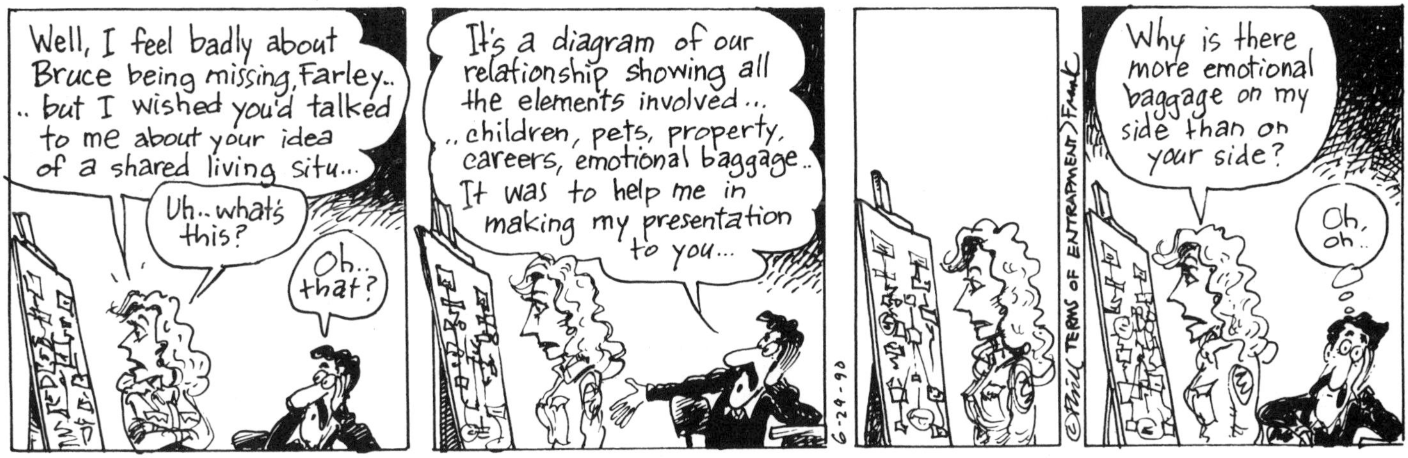
Well, I feel badly about Bruce being missing, Farley.. .. but I wished you'd talked to me about your idea of a shared living situ...
Uh.. what's this?
Oh.. that?
It's a diagram of our relationship showing all the elements involved... ..children, pets, property, careers, emotional baggage.. It was to help me in making my presentation to you...
6-24-90
©Phil Frank (TERMS OF ENTRAPMENT)
Why is there more emotional baggage on my side than on your side?
Oh, oh..

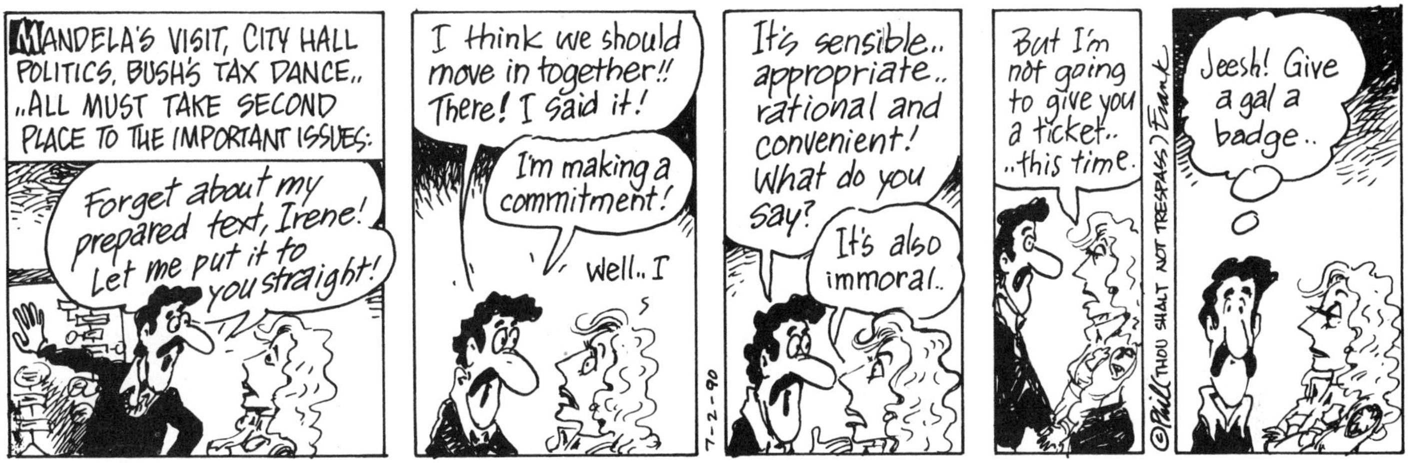
MANDELA'S VISIT, CITY HALL POLITICS, BUSH'S TAX DANCE.. ..ALL MUST TAKE SECOND PLACE TO THE IMPORTANT ISSUES:
Forget about my prepared text, Irene! Let me put it to you straight!
I think we should move in together!! There! I said it!
I'm making a commitment!
Well.. I
7-2-90
It's sensible.. appropriate.. rational and convenient! What do you say?
It's also immoral..
But I'm not going to give you a ticket.. ..this time.
©Phil Frank (THOU SHALT NOT TRESPASS)
Jeesh! Give a gal a badge..

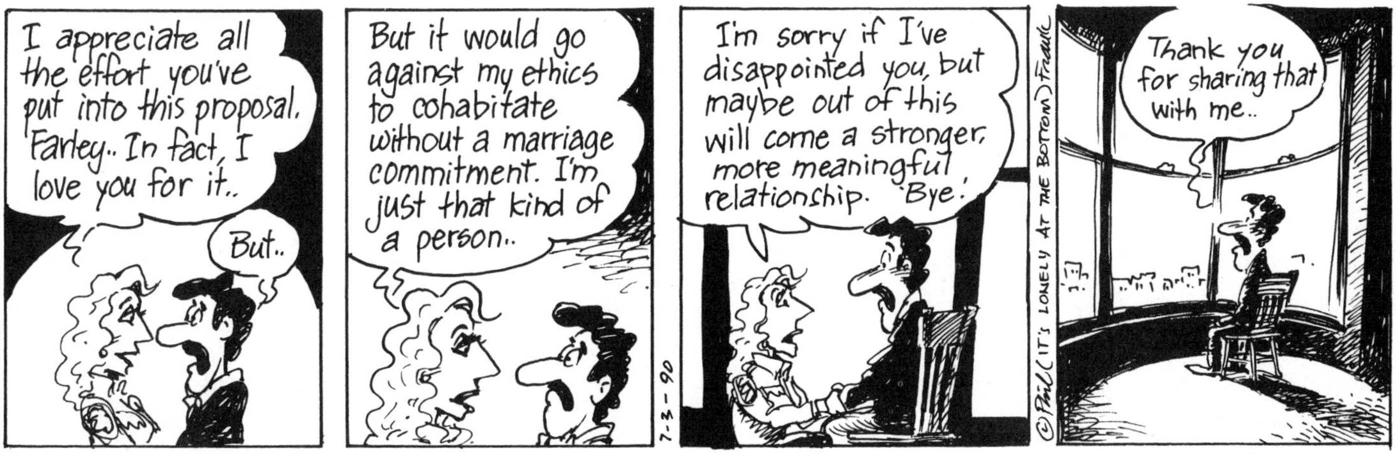
I appreciate all the effort you've put into this proposal, Farley.. In fact, I love you for it..
But..
But it would go against my ethics to cohabitate without a marriage commitment. I'm just that kind of a person..
7-3-90
I'm sorry if I've disappointed you, but maybe out of this will come a stronger, more meaningful relationship. 'Bye!
©Phil Frank (IT'S LONELY AT THE BOTTOM)
Thank you for sharing that with me..

Oh, I have slipped the surly bonds of Earth.. And danced the skies on laughter-silvered wings;

A year previous to the appearance of this series, I had the opportunity to spend a week on the Farallon Islands off the Marin coast as a volunteer with the Point Reyes Bird Observatory. Bruce had been suffering from urban overload so I thought I'd send him to the islands in search of his lady love. All the bird information in the series is based on the recorded history of raven activity on the islands.

OUT OF THE GREY, DRAB VALLEYS OF THE CITY RISES A BIRD.. BURDENED BY THE VAGARIES OF URBAN LIFE..

Get me outta here!

6-23-90

Diesel bus fumes.. a congested city.. honking horns.. pet owners with their weird emotional hang-ups.. Who needs it?

BELOW HIM THE PARK.. THEN THE SUNSET DISTRICT.. AND THE CLIFF HOUSE, THE LAST VESTIGE OF THE HAND OF MAN..

WINGS.. DO YOUR THING! ©Frank

OUT TO SEA WHERE THE SALT AIR AND OCEAN BECKONS AND OFF IN THE DISTANCE.... THE FARALLONES AND SOLACE.

To paraphrase Shakespeare: "Get thee to the rookery"

S.P.C.A.? Yes.. I have a missing bird.' No... ..I don't **have** it. He's mine...But he's gone. I've looked everywhere. He's vanished!!

MEANWHILE, OUT AT SEA:

Oh, I have slipped the surly bonds of Earth.. And danced the skies on laughter-silvered wings;

6-26-90

Yes.. He's a raven.. ..black, no markings.. except a friendship bracelet from a Bohemian Waxwing. Wingspan? Three feet.

Sunward I've climbed and joined the tumbling mirth Of sun-split clouds and done a hundred things You have not dreamed of..

EXTRA ANCHOVIES! ©Frank

Name? Bruce But he won't respond to it! You have to say "PIZZA"! That's right.. "PIZZA".. P.. I.. Z...

Row 1

Panel 1:
FARLEY'S ON THE PHONE TO THE S.P.C.A.
Well.. If you find him, let me know. You have my number. Thank you.

Panel 2:
WHILE NOT FAR FROM THE FARALLON ISLANDS:
High in the sunlit silence Hov'ring there, I've chased the shouting wind along and flung myself through footless halls of air..

Panel 3:
It's all my fault. I was too harsh. He must be so upset..

6-27-90

Panel 4:
Up, up the long delirious, burning blue I've topped the windswept height with easy grace, Where never lark or even eagle flew..

© Phil ("WORM BOY" IN THE FIFTH!) Frank

Panel 5:
I'll keep his cage just as he left it. (SNIFF!).. ..racing form and all.. (SNIFF!)

Row 2

Panel 1:
(A) BIOLOGIST WITH THE POINT REYES BIRD OBSERVATORY IS STANDING WATCH AT THE FARALLON ISLANDS' LIGHTHOUSE:
I'VE GOT A BOGEY AT 3 O'CLOCK!!

7-5-90

Panel 2:
It's an incoming raven.. ..on a direct route from San Francisco!

Panel 3:
What's our last reported sighting of a raven out here? Over.
Uh... appears to be 1974.. ..a female.. over.

© Phil (THE BERMUDA RECTANGLE) Frank

Panel 4:
Hope she hasn't stood me up..

Row 3

Panel 1:
THE BIRD ALARM IS SOUNDED ON THE FARALLON ISLANDS:
BONG! BONG! BONG!
Raven sighted! Raven sighted! First one in sixteen years!!

Panel 2:
IT WAS TRUE! THERE ON A CLIFF AMIDST A HORDE OF WESTERN GULLS, PUFFINS, COMMON MURRES AND CASSIN'S AUCKLETS STOOD AN OUT-OF-PLACE RAVEN:
Hey! What's happenin', guys?

7-10-90

Panel 3:
Appears to be a male. He's in the seagull rookery on the east side of Saddle Rock!

Panel 4:
Sure you haven't seen her? Black feathers.. ..bit shorter than me. she was here in '74. I just went to the City to get a cup of coffee.. and.. well..

© Phil (GROUNDS FOR DIVORCE) Frank

Hello! **Fat Boy Pizza!** We deliver anywhere in the area within one hour or your pizza is free.

May I take your order?

One large Mediterranean **Combo**... with extra anchovies.. Got it.

What address would that be delivered to?

Farallones.

Let's see.. Farallones.. Farallones.. Is that in the Outer Sunset?

Waaaaay Outer Sunset!

WHILE HE'S HAPPY TO HAVE THE ISOLATION OF THE **FARALLONES** ROOKERY, BRUCE LEARNS THERE ARE CERTAIN DRAWBACKS:

I can't believe you birds have to drag all your food way out here!

You can haul **your** food out here from the mainland dumps if you want to...

..but not **this** dude!

MEANWHILE, SKIMMING LOW ACROSS THE WATER, A CALIFORNIA BROWN PELICAN APPROACHES THE ISLANDS FROM THE EAST.

Fat Boy Pizza delivery. You Bruce?

Wow! And in a warming pouch, no less!

ON HIS ISOLATION ON THE **FARALLONES**, BRUCE BEGINS TO REMINISCE FONDLY ABOUT HIS OWNER BACK ON THE MAINLAND:

Hmmm

Maybe I **was** a little rough on him at times..

Like when he had that dream..

It was great for my male ego, Bruce. I was walking down this street with a gorgeous woman on each arm..

Gee.. I'm surprised..

Why?

You said you'd never get tattoos!

AWWK!

Hee! Hee! Hee! I'm so bad!!

Bay Area birdwatchers are in a tizzy! The first raven to make its way to the Farallon Islands in 16 years has been sighted! We now go to Juan Escobar!

We are anchored off the island, Wendy. This **is** a bird sanctuary. This is as close as we can get..

But here **is** a shot of the raven.. standing out in solitary isolation among the sea gulls. He looks lost and very lonely..

Before the 1974 raven spotting... what was the previous sighting, Juan?

In 1903, Wendy, there was a pair. The lighthouse keeper shot them. BRUCE!

©Paul CALLOUS IN WONDERLAND) Frank

FARLEY IS IN TOUCH WITH THE FARALLON ISLANDS VIA SHORT WAVE RADIO FROM THE **POINT REYES BIRD OBSERVATORY**:

The raven on your island... ..can you see him now? Over.

Roger! I have him in sight now. Over!

Is he wearing a friendship bracelet on his right leg?

7-12-90

Affirmative. Blue on red. He looks a little lost in the sea gull rookery. Over.

Great! What is he doing with gulls? Over.

©Paul BERMUDA SCHWARTZ) Frank

Looks like he's playing **Three Card Monte** with them. Over.

Roger! That's him. Over and out.

TIME WEARS HEAVY ON OUR RAVEN IN HIS LONELY SOLITUDE ON THE **FARALLONES**. HE HOPES BEYOND HOPE THAT HIS MATE WILL RETURN.

SUDDENLY, IN THE DISTANCE.. HE SPOTS A FAMILIAR SHAPE WINGING ITS WAY FROM THE MAINLAND.

7-25-90

COULD IT BE A DOUBLE-CRESTED CORMORANT?.. A MERGANSER? A RED-TAILED HAWK?.. A COMMON MURRE?

No!! It's... It's.. It's..

©Paul NERD'S EYE VIEW) Frank

Babycakes!!

HIS WAIT FOR HIS FORMER MATE'S ARRIVAL IS OVER. BRUCE RISES TO THE OCCASION.

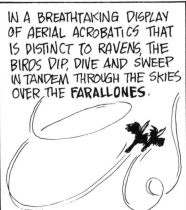
IN A BREATHTAKING DISPLAY OF AERIAL ACROBATICS THAT IS DISTINCT TO RAVENS, THE BIRDS DIP, DIVE AND SWEEP IN TANDEM THROUGH THE SKIES OVER THE **FARALLONES**.

7-26-90

THEIR GRACEFUL SKY DANCE DRAWS ADMIRING STARES FROM BIRDS AND BIRDWATCHERS ALIKE ON THE ISLAND..

©Phil(TALON SEARCH)Frank

.. WHO CAN ONLY WONDER ABOUT THE MARVELOUS COMMUNICATION BETWEEN THE TWO ACROBATS.

Who's the friendship bracelet from, Bruce?

I can explain that.

8-3-90

Two problems I have when it comes to a nest full of baby birds, sweetheart.

They're ugly as sin and they're always hungry.

BRUCE!! shame on you!

How many of those little bug-eaters did we hatch out?

Thirty-four out of the nest in twelve sittings.

We incubated, hatched, fed, cleaned, loved and educated each and every one and sent them on their way.. ...(sigh!)..

(Sigh!)

©Phil(Nary a peep)Frank

And do any of those thirty-four bums write or call their mother? Never!

Kids!

The ravens wing their way to their rookery...
...the bears put up a new "Special of the Day" at the Fog City Dumpster... Irene tickets a double-parked socialite on Post Street... Baba cleans his crystal ball with Windex... Farley stares at the blank screen of his video terminal, trying to meet the deadline at the Daily Requirement and life, as we have come to know it, goes on.